THIS BOOK
BELONGS TO

_____

In with the Old

IN WITH THE OLD

CLASSIC DÉCOR *from* A TO Z

JENNIFER BOLES

PHOTOGRAPHY BY ERICA GEORGE DINES

ILLUSTRATIONS BY LAURA BOLES FAW

POTTER STYLE
NEW YORK

To Billy Baldwin, Eleanor McMillen Brown, Madeleine Castaing, Rose Cumming, Elsie de Wolfe, Angelo Donghia, Dorothy Draper, Frances Elkins, John Fowler, Michael Greer, Albert Hadley, Mark Hampton, David Hicks, Nancy Lancaster, Syrie Maugham, William Pahlmann, Sister Parish, Van Day Truex, Ruby Ross Wood, and all of the other design legends of the past, whose work continues to inspire and dazzle me still today.

Published in the United States by Potter Style, an imprint of the Crown Publishing Group, a division of Random House, Inc., New York.
www.crownpublishing.com
www.clarksonpotter.com

Potter Style is a registered trademark of Random House, Inc.

Library of Congress Cataloging-in-Publication Data
Boles, Jennifer.
    In with the old / Jennifer Boles.
        pages cm
1. Interior decoration—History—20th century—Themes, motives.   I. Title.
    NK1980.B65 2013
    747—dc232013002756

ISBN 978-0-385-34516-3
eISBN 978-0-385-34517-0

Printed in China

Book and cover design by Rae Ann Spitzenberger
Cover illustrations by Laura Boles Faw

10 9 8 7 6 5 4 3 2 1

First Edition

CONTENTS

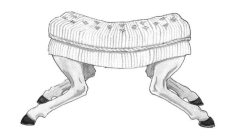

FOREWORD

THERE IS ONLY ONE GUARANTEED WAY TO BECOME A MASTER AT any discipline: to be a master, you must master the material. As a perpetual student of design, I am always amazed by how much good design has been pioneered in the past and I love lingering on the work of the greats and relearning the lessons visible in their practices. I love, equally, perusing the work of present-day designers, especially those whose mastery of their profession and of the subject is obvious. Perhaps the one thing that has worried me over the years is how to sort through the growing glut of images and information out there in this digital age, where everything is to be had and to be seen. How could anyone ever begin to cull and share all of the important images in the hope of showing their examples and exemplars? And how are we to capture and advocate for our historical trove of images, so that it doesn't drown in the swell of current work?

Well I, for one, thank the heavens above for *The Peak of Chic*'s Jennifer Boles. She is now my design historian and my design information curator. With her editorial eye, love of the past, and incredible ability to extract knowledge from images full of cacophonous data—and her transparent joy for her work—Boles has become both the author and the guardian of the new interior design canon. In anyone's opinion, this is no small feat. And her accomplishments inspire many heartfelt responses. Sometimes my love for her eye is pure: she introduces me to designs I have never seen, that are pristine, and from which she concludes ideas that are profound. Sometimes my love for her eye is profane, when I vainly congratulate myself for having a shared love for an interior designer whose praises she is extolling. No matter which response she evokes, though, I am always engaged by what she has to say.

The most remarkable aspect of Boles's ability to assemble and analyze her garden of earthly delights is that as she does it she takes her reader much further into an experience than can be simply explained by displaying images and describing what they show. This book is a rare treasure. On every page Boles invites you to submerge yourself into the era in which these designs thrived, to observe and absorb the customs of the days of their creation. Her writing brings you into the world of her subjects and their milieu, as well draws attention to all of the details. As a result, she creates an almost tangible experience that triggers a sense memory—if you've never lived with chintz or upholstered doors, after reading *In with the Old,* at the very least you'll feel that perhaps you should. Boles teaches us about design, but she also teaches us history, fashion, manners, and style. And, by example, Boles shows us how to love learning about design. Her passion for the topic and her vast store of exhaustive knowledge have made her an ultimate master of her domain.

—ALEXA HAMPTON,
author of *Alexa Hampton: The Language of
Interior Design* and *Decorating in Detail*

INTRODUCTION

CLASSIC DESIGN NEVER GOES OUT OF STYLE, WHETHER IN FASHION (think of Audrey Hepburn's little black dress in *Breakfast at Tiffany's*) or interior decorating. If you cull through centuries' worth of furniture, fabrics, and decorative details, you'll find a wealth of designs that have transcended the ages thanks to their utterly simple lines and shapes, for example, or their perennial good looks and flair. After all, just because the klismos chair can trace its roots to the ancient world, it doesn't mean that it's an outdated relic. In fact, the klismos chair remains one of the most modern-looking chairs, something perhaps attributed to its restrained design. And what about toile? Yes, it's a traditional fabric, but it can look rather daring when rendered in bright colors and present-day scenes, making it a bold counterpart to contemporary furnishings. And therein lies the secret to decorating with traditional elements: sometimes something old requires a little tweaking, through color, finish, or scale, to transform it into something altogether new.

Decorating and gracious living have always played significant roles in my life, something that I attribute to my Southern upbringing, my house-proud parents, and my family's decorator, a true Southern eccentric of great style and maddening business practices. But it wasn't until an all-night reading marathon of designer Dorothy Draper's now-classic *Decorating Is Fun!,* that my interest in design history piqued. I marveled that a 1939 how-to decorating guide could inspire me while still providing useful information decades after it had been written. Thanks to Dorothy's upbeat book, I set out to learn as much as I could about interiors and designers from yesteryear and began collecting a vast library of out-of-print design books. In 2006 I started my design blog, *The Peak of Chic,* so that I could share my knowledge with a wider audience and keep the legacies of the design greats alive.

During my years of research, I have been dazzled by Cole Porter's glamorous Manhattan apartment, which Billy Baldwin fabulously decorated and appointed with mirrored walls, brass bookcases, and tortoiseshell walls. I fell under the spell of "The Dean of American Decorators," Albert Hadley, whose work from the 1960s and '70s still looks modern—a feat considering how quickly trends come and go. After years of studying photos of these old interiors, I came to realize that many vintage rooms are chock-full of great design ideas, there for the taking if only one approaches them with an open mind and a discerning eye.

This book compiles the most classic, charming decorative elements from the past and presents them for today. Here you'll learn about slipper chairs, banquettes, and bar carts, all of which make one's home party-ready. And ideas for injecting glamour into one's home are woven throughout this book, from satin and rock crystal to mirrored rooms and malachite. If an entry in this book sparks your imagination, by all means have a go at it and incorporate it into your home. Don't be reluctant to experiment simply because your friends and neighbors don't collect porcelain or have trompe l'oeil wallpaper in their homes. In fact, that's even more of a reason to do so, because these decorative notions will season your home with a personality that is all your own. As Billy Baldwin so aptly put it, "The ultimate result should be a room where you are surrounded by the things that really make you comfortable and happy, things that you really love."

ACRYLIC

WHETHER YOU KNOW IT AS LUCITE, PLEXIGLAS, OR PERSPEX, ACRYLIC, the ingenious clear plastic that was introduced to the public over eighty years ago, initially caused quite a stir among designers, stoking their fertile imaginations and resulting in some rather outlandish furniture. In the 1930s, skincare impresario Helena Rubinstein, who was often found at the forefront of daring design trends, commissioned an acrylic bed with an illuminated head- and footboard, one that played host to her morning business meetings. By the 1950s, however, acrylic had matured, and it was being used in more practical household items like lamps and barware. But it was a furniture designer of Venetian nobility, the late Baron Alessandro Albrizzi, who conjured up some of the most dazzling acrylic pieces ever designed. His contemporary acrylic tables, storage cubes, and backgammon sets were all the rage among the 1960s-era beautiful people, and in fact, his work is still highly sought after today.

Acrylic is versatile, thanks in no small part to its transparency. Whether you add acrylic furniture to a room outfitted with travertine floors and Damien Hirst art or with an Aubusson rug and Renoir paintings, it won't upset your room's décor because it will blend in visually with its surroundings. And more important, because acrylic is

A Lucite waterfall table, one of the more popular styles of acrylic furniture, strikes a modern note that harmonizes with both contemporary and traditional furnishings. Thanks to its transparency, it has substance without visual bulk.

ACRYLIC IS VERSATILE, THANKS IN NO SMALL PART TO ITS TRANSPARENCY.

crystal clear, it lacks visual heft, providing a seemingly weightless counterpoint to a room's chunkier furniture.

Let's say you have a large upholstered sofa and two plump armchairs in your living room. To this arrangement, you'll of course want to add a cocktail table that is large enough to hold books and objects. And yet what this grouping doesn't need is a bulky-looking table that will make your room look overweight. Instead, try using an acrylic coffee table, whether it has a classic waterfall shape or it has a decorative base. Not only will the acrylic table lighten up the space but its sleek, shiny surface will also impart some polish to the room. (New York–based Plexi-Craft is a great source for acrylic tables, not to mention étagères, magazine racks, and serving trays too.)

The same goes for chairs. Have you ever realized that what you really need in your living room is additional seating, but the room doesn't look like it can possibly hold one more piece of furniture? Introduce an acrylic klismos chair or two or perhaps one of designer Philippe Starck's aptly named Louis Ghost chairs. These plastic perches will practically vanish before your eyes, yet not without supporting your room's, and your guests', bottom line.

SEE ALSO
*Klismos
Chairs.*

ANDIRONS
AND CHENETS

CONSIDERING THAT THE FIREPLACE PROVIDES SUCH WARMTH AND coziness for all who surround it, shouldn't it be lavished with as much attention as the rest of a room? As Edith Wharton and Ogden Codman Jr. wrote in their legendary treatise on tasteful design, *The Decoration of Houses,* "The effect of a fireplace depends much upon the good taste and appropriateness of its accessories." And few fireplace accessories are as useful or decorative as the andiron.

Just as we need air to survive, so too does fire. In order for wooden logs to burn efficiently, they have to be raised off the ground so that air can pass beneath them. Otherwise, you're going to end up with a smoky mess. A pair of andirons, which are basically upright decorative ornaments attached to sturdy horizontal iron bars, will give your firewood a resting place upon which to burn. Chenets, by the way, are a type of andiron, French in origin and usually ornate in style.

Because andiron styles run the gamut, finding a pair to match your décor has never been easier. A mountain house filled with rustic antiques is the perfect venue for a pair of

Traditional brass andirons look like shiny gleaming sentries keeping watch over a roaring fire, providing both decorative swagger and practical support to the fireplace in which they stand.

SEE ALSO
Rock Crystal.

traditional iron and brass andirons. Do you live in a city home with an opulent sensibility? Ormolu chenets dripping in rococo swirls should do the trick. If you're a person who never misses an opportunity to indulge in a little humor, seek out a pair of vintage cast iron andirons in the shape of owls or cats, both of which were usually made with glass marble eyes. When you light a fire, the eyes of your andirons will look as though they have come to life, though I admit in a possessed kind of way. Or seek out dazzling andirons made of rock crystal—so posh, and yet so practical.

If andirons and chenets are like jewelry for the fireplace, then consider adding a few more accessories to complete the ensemble. There are the obvious tools necessary for stoking fires, not to mention those metal mesh or glass fire screens that protect nearby rugs from errant embers. Also serving a similar purpose are fenders, which can best be described as metal bumpers for your fireplace. If you want to give your fireplace a British accent, invest in a club fender, which looks like a brass bench with an upholstered leather top. Seen around many an English fireplace, the club fender provides a seat upon which to warm your hands and feet. Now what's cozier than that?

B | BALLROOM CHAIRS

FEW SOCIALITES ARE AS UBIQUITOUS ON THE PARTY CIRCUIT AS the ballroom chair. Whether it was a Gilded Age ball or a Paris couture show in the 1950s, the ballroom chair was probably there, its often-gilded frame providing welcome seating for weary guests. But in spite of its party-animal reputation, ballroom chairs can be homebodies too.

Although the Chiavari-style ballroom chair, famous for its turned legs and back that resemble knotty bamboo, is ever-present at weddings and special events, it also lends itself for use at home where its small size and light weight prove versatile and practical.

The most common type of ballroom chair is the Chiavari chair, which has back splats and legs made of turned wood that, in a way, resemble bamboo. Chiavari chairs can be purchased at party supply stores or online for less than $50 apiece. Did I mention that these chairs come in an array of colors? Gold, silver, black, white, red, and natural are just a few of the off-the-shelf options, although these chairs can be custom-painted as well. For those who march to a contempo beat, Chiavari chairs are made in materials other than wood, like acrylic, resin, and brass.

Because of their modest size, ballroom chairs fit right in—literally—with the rest of your home's furnishings. Do

SEE ALSO
Acrylic;
Bamboo;
Dressing
Rooms.

you own an antique desk with a narrow kneehole? A commercial office chair wouldn't be a good match, but a small ballroom chair might be. A pretty gilt or acrylic Chiavari chair looks smashing when partnered with a dressing table, especially when its cushion is covered in silk or velvet. And tuck a chair or two in your living room's corners or niches, where they will serve as discreet spare chairs, at the ready should they be invited to join the party.

It's in the dining room, of course, where ballroom chairs can be at their most hospitable. If you can't afford that set of antique dining chairs you've been coveting, buy a set of ballroom chairs in a color that matches your room's décor. Who knows? What started out as a stopgap measure might turn into something more permanent.

 WHAT A SWELL PARTY IT WAS

Some of the twentieth century's grandest soirées were affairs to remember because of their inspired themes, high-wattage guests, and over-the-top décor.

THE CIRCUS BALL: Although Elsie de Wolfe played hostess at her 1938 circus-themed fête, it was designer Stéphane Boudin of Maison Jansen who conjured up both a green-and-white-striped dance pavilion and a tree trunk–wrapped champagne bar. The icing on the cake? Acrobats and tightrope walkers who frolicked among guests.

THE ORIENTAL BALL: The Baron de Redé hosted his 1969 Oriental costume party at his impeccable Paris hôtel particulier, but thanks to designers Valerian Rybar and Jean-François Daigre, the scene was reminiscent of Arabian Nights—especially the life-size, papier-mâché elephants and bare-chested male torchbearers who greeted guests.

PERSEPOLIS CELEBRATION: Hosted by the Shah of Iran and his wife, this 1971 four-day extravaganza, which was designed by Maison Jansen, marked the 2,500th anniversary of the founding of Persia. Sumptuously appointed tents, D. Porthault linen, Limoges china, and meals prepared by Maxim's made this party a legend, but some say it also led to the shah's downfall.

B | BAMBOO

HARKENING BACK TO THE CHINOISERIE CRAZE OF EIGHTEENTH-century Europe, bamboo, or more specifically a stylized imitation of it, has been a popular decorative motif for an abundance of furnishings. For centuries, wooden table and chair legs have been carved or turned to simulate knotty stalks of bamboo, with painted faux finishes often being added to further heighten the illusionary effect. Metal, too, has been crafted into some semblance of bamboo, with some of the most notable examples having been made by famed French metal crafters Maison Baguès. Their gilt and brass bamboo tables, bar carts, and lamps were the dernier cri of mid-twentieth-century design and are still considered so today. I'll go out on a limb to say that vintage Baguès pieces practically seem a requirement for today's fashionable abodes from Manhattan to Paris.

I'll leave the details of the Royal Pavilion, King George IV's pleasure palace in Brighton, England, to the entry on "Chinoiserie," but suffice it to say, the palace interiors were tricked out in a profusion of bamboo motifs, something that has since spawned a plethora of bamboo-themed wallpaper. Three of my favorite prints are Scalamandré's Baldwin Bamboo, Bamboo Grill by Clarence House, and Petite Pavilion by Inez Croom. Because bamboo print wallpapers tend to be

SEE ALSO
Chinoiserie.

busy looking, they're best used in compact spaces like entry halls, powder rooms, or breakfast nooks. You could forgo papering walls altogether and choose instead to paper a room's ceiling, an effect that is unexpected yet chic.

Why not a bamboo-style mirror? I recently saw one that was custom-made by a local designer, and I thought it very clever. The designer visited his local framer, where he purchased bamboo picture frame molding, each piece cut to his size specifications. He then glued the molding directly to a mirrored fireplace overmantel, creating a geometric pattern that was meant to evoke the style of my favorite great lady decorator, the late Dorothy Draper. Not only did he succeed, but I think that Draper would have applauded the designer's stylish ingenuity.

It's on the dining table, however, where bamboo is in abundance. The most iconic flatware pattern of the twentieth century was Tiffany & Co.'s Bamboo, created by legendary designer Van Day Truex. With each utensil handle crafted to resemble a silver bamboo stalk, the Bamboo pattern was widely imitated, perhaps a good thing considering that Tiffany has since discontinued its classic pattern. If you set a more casual table, you might want to consider investing in a set of flatware with bamboo-style handles made of wood or resin. Then there is china with rims resembling bamboo and napkins with embroidered bamboo, not to mention bamboo-like candlesticks made of glass, silver, or ceramic. With such beguiling choices, it's tempting to get bamboozled.

Scalamandré's Baldwin Bamboo wallpaper is splashed across the walls of this ladies' powder room while a curvy loop chair stands at the ready. Although such a profusion of the bamboo motif could have been distracting, the paper's pale lettuce and cream color combination tones down the print's intensity.

B | BANQUETTES

AFTER YEARS OF STUDYING PHOTOS OF SOCIAL SWELLS' HOMES, ritzy restaurants, luxurious lounges, and even London's notoriously private clubs (captured surreptitiously), I have noticed they almost always have one thing in common: the banquette. It's funny how an armless upholstered sofa ended up with such social and stylish clout.

The banquette's prevalence in restaurants and clubs might be explained by its lack of sides and arms, allowing it to be built as narrow or as wide as needed. Depending on its size, a banquette can accommodate two or twenty. Dimensions aside, upholstered banquettes are usually quite comfortable. Wouldn't you prefer to take your cocktails on something akin to a sofa rather than a hard little chair?

Because they usually come with straight backs, banquettes work best when placed against a wall, allowing for seating along a room's periphery. If you live in small quarters, a living room banquette makes sense because it can hug the wall rather than cause congestion in the middle of the room. And the other asset of a banquette—one of its best, I think—is that it can be built to fit into awkward spaces where seating is often a challenge—namely, a room's corners, recesses, and alcoves. Is it any wonder that the banquette is beloved by social types who like to squeeze as many people into a room as possible?

Obviously, you should upholster a banquette in a fabric that is in keeping with the room's other décor. However, keep in mind that because a banquette can have decadent sensibilities, especially when it encourages guests to lounge, gossip, and let loose, it often looks its best when covered in a sumptuous fabric. Some of the most inviting versions I have seen are those in luxurious velvet, mohair, or silk. One of my favorite photos of Marella Agnelli, the Italian socialite who was one of Truman Capote's fabled swans, shows her dressed to the nines in a chiffon evening gown and enormous chandelier earrings while seated near a long mint-green silk banquette laden with coordinated silk throw pillows. Now that's chic.

Don't forget that your guests will need a spot to park their drinks, so place a small table or two in front of your banquette. Delicate tables, like those with spindly gilt or brass legs and glass tops, work nicely to balance the banquette's heft. And do as Marella Agnelli did and scatter throw pillows onto your banquette to maximize comfort. After all, this is not the kind of seating that requires one to sit up straight.

Keep in mind that just as in restaurants, banquettes can also be used in lieu of chairs in kitchens, breakfast nooks, and dining rooms. If you use your banquette for dining, upholster it in a durable fabric that can withstand food and drink spills. You may also want to avoid tufting, as you'll have a devil of a time vacuuming up crumbs.

One last thing: while a custom-built banquette may be necessary for some spaces, it's not a requirement for most. There are many furniture companies that sell banquettes in a variety of sizes and fabrics. You're sure to find one that fits your home and your budget.

An upholstered banquette, which wraps around the corner of a room, is a luxurious retreat for a gossip-charged confab or a discreet tête à tête. Soft fabrics, like velvet, and scattered throw pillows create a sense of coziness, while a small cocktail table provides an essential surface for drinks.

B | BAR CARTS AND BUTLER'S TRAYS

UP UNTIL A FEW DECADES AGO, PROPER ENTERTAINING CALLED FOR three- (sometimes even four!) course meals, dinner jackets and hostess gowns, and cocktails mixed at a bar cart. Mercifully, we no longer feel the pressure to prepare such elaborate meals. And while the days of the hostess gown may have come and gone, it's reassuring to know that the bar cart is just as popular today as it ever was.

For special occasions such as an afternoon birthday celebration, I clear my bar cart of its usual stock of spirits and mixers and fill it with party necessities. Bottles of rosé champagne, pink macarons, pistachio dragées, and fuchsia cocktail napkins all but guarantee a festive time.

Traditionally, a bar cart has multiple shelves for holding liquor, mixers, and accessories plus a handle and wheels that allow the cart to be pushed wherever needed. Basic structure aside, bar carts, both vintage and newer versions, come in a dazzling array of designs and finishes. Thankfully, there is a bar car fit for every personality, and every type of cocktail too.

Are you a fan of classic libations like the martini, the Manhattan, or even pink gin? If so, a glamorous chrome and mirrored bar cart is the one for you. Do you prefer Brandy Alexanders or Harvey Wallbangers? By all means, stick with the 1970s theme and go with something groovy like a brass, Lucite, or smoked glass cart. And if you're a single-malt scotch–drinking Anglophile, consider one of those proper mahogany and brass versions that looks straight out of an English gentlemen's club.

One advantage of a bar cart is that you can wheel it to the room where the party is taking place, whether that be the living room, the study, or even the patio. Whatever you do, though, make sure to place the cart in the desired room before the party begins. If you start pushing it around your guests, it's likely to remind them of being on an airplane. (And the same goes if you serve your guests those miniature-size bottles of alcohol too.)

The secret of all good hosts and hostesses is that, like Boy Scouts, they know to be prepared. If you entertain often, you will find that a bar cart that is always at the ready will make your life a lot easier. Leave your bar cart set up at all times in the room where you tend to gather with guests. Make sure that you always have the necessary liquors, mixers, cocktail glasses, and other cocktail accoutrements on hand. That way, your only task before your guests arrive is to simply fill an ice bucket with ice.

If you live in small quarters and cannot devote the floor space to a bar cart, you do have other options. Butler's trays are very handy and can be employed for bar setups at parties. When not in use, the handled tray and foldable base can be stowed away easily in a closet. Also, a large tray placed on a side table or console is an elegant and practical way to hold one's decanters and glassware.

Finally, don't think that bar carts and butler's trays are meant only for beverage service. If after dinner you enjoy taking dessert in your living room, why not treat your bar cart like a tea trolley from which to serve coffee and sweets? If you're in need of a bedside table, try using a butler's tray. Its folding legs don't take up much space, yet the tray is large enough to hold all of your bedside necessities. And while at first it might seem incongruous, you can even use a bar cart in your bathroom to hold bath towels and linen.

B | BLANC DE CHINE

LOOK CLOSELY AT MOVIE SETS FROM THE 1920S AND 1930S, AND you'll often see white porcelain figurines that were displayed on wall brackets or tabletops. These figurines, usually depicting traditionally dressed Chinese women or men, are referred to as *blanc de chine,* meaning "white of china." The reason for their popularity on old movie sets is much the same as it is today: blanc de chine porcelain adds decoration without introducing conflicting color or pattern to a room.

Because of the primitive film technology of the time, early movies, shot in black and white, of course, required sets that were decorated in varying shades of whites. Set designers had to employ white fabrics, white paints, white furniture, and white accessories on their sets. And at that time, few white accessories implied sophistication, worldliness, and wealth more than those Asian blanc de chine figures. In real life, thank goodness, things aren't so black and white. We can paint our walls cherry red or upholster our settees in emerald-green velvet. But remember that in a room filled with color, pattern, or copious objects, one's eyes need to have a place to rest, and where better to do so than upon tranquil, milky-white porcelain?

Because blanc de chine pieces are essentially colorless, their aesthetic value lies in their shape and their surface decoration. There are

SEE ALSO
Brackets.

A blanc de chine Guanyin figure might only seem appropriate among hand-painted Chinese wallpaper, but its finish, which is devoid of interfering color, works well with most décor.

the aforementioned, traditional blanc de chine figures of robed Chinese women, known as *guanyin,* not to mention more stylized Art Deco figures too. Birds, urns, and lamps have been crafted from this glazed white porcelain, as has dinnerware, whose blank white surface won't compete with the food served on it. And because white goes with anything, blanc de chine marries well with hypercontemporary pieces just as it does with those furnishings that have a little (or a lot of) age to them. In spite of today's "anything goes" approach to design, it's blanc de chine's purity that has remained its strongest virtue.

 SILVER SCREEN STYLE

Although old movie sets were often fantasy worlds of penthouses and luxury ocean liners, their high-style swagger and dashing details can be easily adapted for real-life interiors too.

TOP HAT (1935)—Fred Astaire and Ginger Rogers dance their way cheek-to-cheek from London to Venice, encountering dramatic-looking floors, fanciful gondolas, and feather-trimmed satin gowns.

MY MAN GODFREY (1936)—What's not to covet about the film's plaster wall ornamentation, white klismos chairs, blanc de chine porcelain, and Godfrey, the debonair butler played by William Powell?

ROPE (1948)—There are enough elegant antiques, modern paintings, and champagne coupes in this fictional apartment to make you forget that two murderers live there.

HARRIET CRAIG (1950)—Type A personality Harriet Craig, fittingly played by Joan Crawford, is ruthless in her quest for domestic perfection. Her most treasured possession is a priceless Ming vase.

INDISCREET (1958)—This romantic comedy stars Cary Grant and Ingrid Bergman, whose London flat is a lesson in cozy sophistication. Hit the pause button whenever the camera pans to the framed artwork in the living room. Each piece is framed with a different brightly colored mat.

AUNTIE MAME (1958)—As Mame and her wardrobe change with the times, so, too, does her mad jumble of a New York apartment, with Oriental exotica, 1930s moderne, and Surrealistic accents making appearances throughout the film.

B | BOOKPLATES

DATING BACK CENTURIES TO WHEN BOOKS WERE AMONG PEOPLE'S most prized, not to mention most costly, possessions, bookplates have long been a way for bibliophiles to identify ownership of their books. Traditionally, bookplates—which are basically personalized labels meant to be adhered to the inside cover of a book—were grandly designed with the owner's name, a family crest or motto, and usually the Latin phrase "Ex libris," which translates to "From the library of."

By the mid-twentieth century, bookplate designs had become less formal and more capricious. Nowhere is this more evident than on the bookplates owned by the Hollywood stars of yesteryear, some of whom were actually erudite. The bookplates used by film legend and notorious recluse Greta Garbo featured her likeness in profile, replete with exaggerated eyelashes, while those used by Bing Crosby appropriately bore a flourish of musical notes. Bette Davis paid tribute to her Scottish terrier by placing an illustration of the dog prominently on her bookplate.

The ultimate luxury in bookplates is to commission a stationer to customize a design for you. If this is the route that you take, spend some time looking at examples of bookplates both online and in a stationery shop's archives to help give you a sense of what you want. If you're ever in the Madison Avenue storefront of venerable stationery firm Mrs.

Bookplates not only mark ownership, they also allow you to customize your books with your distinctive style. I apply these chair-motif bookplates, upon which I have written my name, to the inside covers of my decorative arts-related books.

John L. Strong, ask to see examples of the firm's custom bookplates. You will be amazed.

Bookplates don't have to be expensive though. With a little computer savvy and a trusty printer, you can create your own personalized bookplates using clip art of your choosing. You can print your bookplates onto either self-adhesive labels or, as I would recommend, heavy stock paper. Or you can simply buy preprinted bookplates on which

you'll need to write your name. Just know that with any of the nonadhesive bookplates, you will need to affix them to your books' insides using some type of acid-free glue or paste.

Now, if you're still not convinced that bookplates should be part of your stationery wardrobe, there are other ways to label your books, although I personally don't find these options to be as fetching as bookplates. Library embossers that have been personalized with your name or initials can be used to add a blind-embossed seal to the corner of a book's page. This is how the great design firm Parish-Hadley often identified books in its design library. It's a more subtle way of letting people know that a book belongs to you. You could even take your cue from author Truman Capote, who used a customized ink stamp to mark his books. Talk about no-frills!

And one more thing: forgo adding a bookplate or stamp to rare books or first editions. It will only diminish their value.

B | BOUILLOTTE LAMPS

THE BOUILLOTTE LAMP HAS ONE OF THE MOST AMUSING PEDIGREES of all of the lamps in the world. Named for the eighteenth-century French card game of the same name, the bouillotte lamp was conceived to illuminate a table during a game of cards. Originally lit by candles, though now found wired for electricity, the lamp consisted of two to three candle holders attached to a metal shaft with a dish-shaped base, designed to hold the players' game chips. At the top of the shaft was a metal shade that could be moved up or down with the aid of a screw-type key so that even as the wax candles melted down, the shade continued to cover the flames and shield the players' eyes from harsh light. Clever, no?

Because of its elegant shape and its kinship with an old French card game, the delightful bouillotte lamp is always a safe yet stunning choice rather than a decorative gamble.

While the game of bouillotte may have given way to poker and the like, the bouillotte lamp still remains a perennial favorite, with the great designer Mark Hampton once writing, "I feel it is safe to say that it will never be out of favor." So why is such a lamp, one conceived as task lighting for gamblers, still coveted today? Perhaps the answer lies in the lamp's timeless design. Bouillotte lamps, both antique and new, tend to be made of brass or bronze, although cool-toned silver plate is not uncommon. Just like jewelry, silver and golden accessories never go out of style, their shiny or burnished finishes bestowing an old-fashioned razzle-dazzle to a room. And who isn't just the slightest bit intrigued by the lamp's shallow metal shade, something quite different from the plain or pleated fabric shades found in most of our homes?

SEE ALSO *Tôle.*

I really can't think of a room where a bouillotte lamp is not appropriate. Do you have bookshelves that could benefit from some extra light? Place a small bouillotte lamp on one of the shelf ledges or on a tiny table positioned in front of the shelves. Petite bouillotte lamps also provide atmospheric lighting when placed on countertops in kitchens and butler's pantries. (Design purists might be shocked at the use of a fancy lamp in a utilitarian kitchen, but I see no reason not to up the ante.) When used as a bedside lamp, a larger-size bouillotte lamp can do double duty as a *vide-poche* with its base holding your watch, rings, and pocket change.

Generally speaking, lamps often look their best when used in pairs. Not so with the bouillotte lamp. Because of the lamp's intricate and at times ornate design, one will suffice. If you do own a pair, try to keep enough distance between the two lamps so as to balance out the richness. And back to those metal, or tôle, shades: while the traditional bouillotte shade tends to be painted black, there is no reason why you can't have your shade custom-painted to complement your room's décor. Specialty lampshade stores usually carry these metal shades and can often assist with custom orders. Fabric bouillotte shades are also available, but as with most things, the original, I think, is the best.

B | BRACKETS

WHEN IT COMES TO THE ART OF DISPLAYING ONE'S HEIRLOOMS AND mementos, it seems that no surface is off-limits—and that includes wall surfaces too. We're all familiar with the traditional practice of hanging plates on walls. But if you want to heighten the effect of your decorative wall objects, how about displaying them on wall brackets? These small, ornamental shelves are a clever use of space, not to mention the fact that they give your decorative objects an attractive nest upon which to roost. The range of bracket styles is limitless, from Regency and chinoiserie to Art Deco and Empire. There are even contemporary brackets, quite simple in shape, that are made of acrylic, wood, or stone.

A pair of wall brackets, holding an interesting pair of accessories, of course, looks swell when flanking a large painting or mirror over a fireplace, sofa, or console table. Think of the pair as decorative parentheses that help to emphasize the object between them. If you don't own a blue-chip mirror or work of art, then why not

A grouping of wall brackets, which looks cohesive because of its stylistic likeness, serves as an ornamental support system for one's collection. Traditionally, porcelain—like these Meissen birds—was displayed upon such decorative brackets.

decorate a wall with a large grouping of brackets? The key to a successful cluster of wall ornaments is cohesion. Ideally, both the brackets and the objects they hold should be of a strongly similar style and look. Otherwise, the assemblage is going to look messy and unfocused. However, there is an exception to this design rule. If you are a collector of antique and vintage wall brackets of diverse styles, then you can hang them together on one wall and treat them as an art collection. Just don't clutter the congregation by adding accessories to the brackets' shelves.

You can display any number of decorative accessories on your wall brackets. Urns, shells, fossils, busts, Tang Dynasty horses, and small architectural artifacts are just a few bibelots that I have seen displayed to great effect, but if there is one accessory that seems to be catnip to the fashionable set, it is porcelain birds. Those grandes dames Jayne Wrightsman and the late Nan Kempner both had walls in their homes devoted to groupings of wall brackets upon which were placed ceramic birds by Meissen. The panache of such a grouping is still possible today, but you might need to tweak it for your surroundings. A modern-looking flock of birds of one color, say, white, bright yellow, or pale blue, resting on acrylic brackets will give the impression that your feathered friends are magically floating against your wall.

And if you want the functionality of wall bracket shelves without the intrusion of their appearance, then paint your brackets the same color as your walls so that they visually disappear. David Hicks once covered both a wall and wall brackets in claret-colored velvet. Needless to say, the result was both sumptuous and seamless. I still say, though, that unless you want to drive yourself crazy gluing fabric to an uneven-surfaced bracket, stick to paint.

SEE ALSO
Chinoiserie.

C | CACHEPOTS

PLANTS PROVIDE A MUCH NEEDED BREATH OF FRESH AIR TO A home's interiors—and it's not just due to photosynthesis. Lush leaves and blooming buds have a way of preventing a room from looking uptight. As the late Michael Taylor, the designer responsible for popularizing the "California Look" and its lavish use of indoor trees and plants, once wrote, "Plants have a way of preventing a room from appearing overdecorated."

The only things not so attractive about many plants, though, are the green plastic pots in which they're planted. The late socialite and gardening expert C.Z. Guest thought nothing of displaying plastic potted orchids in her home; however, it should be noted that both Guest and her home were so incredibly chic that she was able to pull off this mix of high and low with aplomb. The rest of us might want to consider placing that plastic pot in a cachepot.

A decorative vessel for potted plants or flowers, the cachepot serves to conceal those typically homely plastic containers in which most plants come, happily making repotting unnecessary.

Its name meaning "to hide the pot" in French, a cachepot is a small decorative container used to hold a potted plant and is meant to be displayed on tabletops and surfaces. There are many styles of cachepots available, from antique porcelain versions to contemporary ceramic ones. If your abode's interiors are a paean to eighteenth-century French décor, you should investigate those reproductions of the famous Sèvres

34

porcelain milk pail used by Marie Antoinette when she played milk-maid at Versailles. A brightly colored flowering plant, say, a pink azalea, would look wonderful in such a container. On the other hand, let's say your style is all steely modernism. If that's the case, seek out an unadorned earthenware cachepot or even one made of brushed metal and employ it to hold a sculptural-looking orchid or succulent.

All kinds of containers can be employed as cachepots. A woven basket, a perennial favorite among designers and style mavens, can provide an interesting contrast to an otherwise formal or sleek space. In his memoirs, Billy Baldwin fondly recalls his friend Pauline de Rothschild's unorthodox placement of a flower-laden wicker basket upon an antique French commode. In Baldwin's own glossy Manhattan living room, a humble wooden basket holding potted tulips successfully held its own against the room's higher-style furniture and accessories. Of course, basket containers are always appropriate in traditional, comfortable interiors like those decorated by the late Sister Parish, who was a fan of baskets for use in both town and country alike.

Silver-plated champagne coolers can do double duty as festive cachepots, and the bonus is that these coolers can often be bought in antique shops and flea markets for a song. Those ubiquitous terra-cotta pots that are available in most nurseries also do a nice job of holding potted plants, and like wooden baskets, terra-cotta can help to tone down a room's fancier features. If you're opposed to terra-cotta's orangey tones, you might consider Dorothy Draper's advice to paint these pots black or white. If you use a container with a drainage hole, place an attractive plate beneath it, so the plant's moisture won't damage your table's surface.

CAMPAIGN FURNITURE

ISN'T IT RATHER AMAZING THAT OUT THE FOG OF WAR—THE EARLY nineteenth-century Napoleonic Wars, to be exact—emerged two decorative trends, campaign furniture and tented rooms, that to this day remain impossibly chic? During Napoléon's time, and even well before that, gentleman army officers maintained on the battlefield some semblance of their upper-class lifestyles, retreating at the end of the day to sumptuously appointed tents. Considering that armies were always on the move, the officers' furnishings had to be portable, which thus prompted the commissioning of furniture that was both deluxe and easy to carry. And so campaign furniture was born.

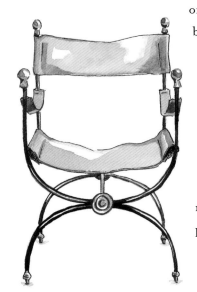

What makes this style of furniture unique is that it's built to be collapsible, with foldable sides and legs that allow the piece to be laid (mostly) flat. Contemporary campaign furniture isn't that radically different from those pieces of Napoléon's era. Chairs, beds, stools, and tables—the furniture most often rendered in the campaign style—were, and still are, typ-

Remarkably similar to those used by Napoléon's army, a metal campaign chair is supported by sturdy yet curvy legs that are foldable and, thus, easy to transport.

ically made of durable steel or wood. For campaign seating, leather or canvas slings attached to both the chair's back and seat provide support. If you think this sounds awfully similar to a director's chair, you are correct. The chair that is so often seen on movie sets, whose back sling is emblazoned with the director's or actor's name, is simply an updated version of the campaign chair.

What's remarkable about campaign furniture is that much like writer Oscar Wilde's character Dorian Gray, it never seems to grow old. The style's clean, simple lines give it a perpetually modern appearance that made it highly valued in the nineteenth century, just as it is today. One of the most noted twentieth-century decorators, the late Michael Greer, flawlessly mixed ornate French antiques with metal campaign chairs and beds, their steely appearance serving as a butch foil to the surrounding feminine, curvy lines. Keep this in mind if you have a room where you need a dose of testosterone.

And in the spirit of "Make love, not war," campaign beds can be a sumptuous retreat or stylish love nest in one's bedroom or sitting room. Seek out a sleek, mid-twentieth-century version (those by Baker Furniture are still in demand) that can be transformed into a twin-size bed or daybed. (Campaign beds tend to be narrow.) Pile the bed with a bevy of throw pillows or bolsters covered in classic ticking, toile, or small geometric prints. You could use the same fabric to cover the room's walls, and while you're at it, you could even drape that fabric behind the campaign bed as a modified canopy. However, I would avoid dressing your campaign bed in too-frilly fabrics adorned with bouquets of flowers, ribbons, or bows. That's akin to dressing a man in a lace slip, and it would not be in keeping with the style's virile origins.

SEE ALSO
Canopies; Geometric Prints; Tented Rooms; Ticking; Toile.

37

CANDLELIGHT

"WHEN ALL IS SAID AND DONE, WE MUST COME BACK TO WAX candles for the most beautiful light of all." Elsie de Wolfe, the early twentieth-century decorator who once expressed this sentiment, should know. After all, she famously quipped that her life's mission would be to make everything around her beautiful. Indeed, not only does candlelight impart a beckoning glow to a room's interior, it also manages to make people look years younger. It might be the latter that explains de Wolfe's affinity for candles.

It's on the dining table where candlelight is practically a requirement. Thankfully, those overwrought candelabra so loved by Liberace seem to be a thing of the past, with today's preference being elegant simplicity. Slim candlesticks strike a statuesque note on one's table and work best for dressier occasions. On the other hand, votives and tea lights complement most table settings because of both their unobtrusive sizes and the variety of materials in which they come, including ceramic, metal, and rock crystal. Because they're inexpensive, there is no reason not to keep plenty of glass votives and votive candles on hand for impromptu dinner parties. (They also look terrific when lining an outdoor walkway at night.)

A chandelier lit solely by candles is a different ball of wax. While

When entertaining at night, a young architect lights his dining room using an antique electric chandelier, candles, and votives. The room's paneled, mirrored windows and the chandelier's crystal drops magnify the candlelight, creating a warm glow.

SEE ALSO
Passementerie;
Valances.

by a canopy with a decorative valance. The secret, though, behind some of Hicks's canopy beds was that they lacked posts. The curtains and fabric canopy were attached directly to the ceiling, giving the illusion of a four-poster bed. Taking Hicks's trick in a slightly different direction, you could attach two decorative curtain rods to the ceiling, one over the head of the bed and the other over the foot, and then drape fabric between the two rods, letting the ends of the fabric hang over the rods. You would have a tailored-looking canopy over your bed, one that required minimal fabric yardage.

Bedsheets can make wonderful curtains for windows, showers, and yes, beds. The noted Washington, D.C., socialite and philanthropist Deeda Blair festooned a canopy-framed bed in her Billy Baldwin–decorated house with her wedding trousseau sheets from D. Porthault. The concoction was frothy, floral, feminine, and fabulous. If you prefer a softly swagged look to your bedsheets-cum-curtains, then tie them to a bed's post with extra-wide ribbon or passementerie tassels.

One last thing: the space within a canopy bed feels like a room to itself, so why not treat it as such? Install two swing-arm reading lamps to the wall behind your bed, and then drape the bed curtains accordingly so that the lamps peek into the canopied room, providing light for reading or surfing the web. Or hang a small decorative mirror or framed art over your bed, positioned in front of the bed curtains. Your canopied bed niche will be so dreamy that you might end up spending most of your waking hours there too.

In this bedroom, a canopied bed was chosen to soften the sloping ceiling between dormers. The sumptuous fabric is attached to the wall and ceiling rather than bed posts, creating a cozy sleeping niche.

CARD MOTIFS

BEFORE THERE WAS COMPUTER SOLITAIRE AND ONLINE POKER, CARD games were something that people played face-to-face while seated at the same table. Throughout most of the last century, card games were a popular form of socializing and entertaining that often included bridge luncheons, afternoon canasta games at the club, and poker nights for husbands seeking a respite from their wives. Not surprisingly, this enthusiasm for cards spilled over into accessories for the home, with the addition of spade, heart, club, and diamond motifs injecting a sense of playfulness to the at-times serious pursuit of cards.

Now discontinued, Tiffany & Co.'s collection of playing card–motif china included dessert plates, seen here, and demitasse sets, both of which were decorated with scattered cards against a black band with a gold rim.

Although the popularity of card games might have reached its zenith in the 1960s, the card suit motif remains a charming decorative vestige of those card-crazy days, one that lends a touch of retro chic to our homes. Demitasse sets and canapé plates, both of which fit easily on card tables, were frequently emblazoned with card suits. Until a few years ago, Tiffany & Co. produced a delightful china pattern with images of playing cards depicted against a black background. Although it has been discontinued, it's worth seeking this card pattern and others on eBay or Etsy or, alternatively, at auction. Cocktail glasses also benefit from etchings or decals of card suits and faces, fitting considering that most card games are now played at night. Playing card motifs are

SEE ALSO
Needlepoint.

even embroidered on table linen and embossed on stationery. How-ever, don't assume that you have to be a card player or even own a card table to enjoy these table accessories. Any of these items, whether new or vintage, provides a playful note to subdued china, glassware, and linen that may lurk in our cabinets.

Card suits and needlepoint seem to go hand in hand, perhaps because both are leisurely pursuits. Style maven Diana Vreeland's liv-ing room sofa boasted needlepoint pillows mimicking the five of hearts and the three of clubs. Needlepoint rugs depicting card suits look quite jolly in rooms not usually reserved for recreation. (Stark Carpet makes a good-looking version.) In the home of the late John Galliher, long considered one of Manhattan's most dapper men, there were not one but five card rugs, although they were hooked, not needlepoint. Believe me when I say there was nothing remotely kitschy about his home. Galliher's rugs were a testament not only to his fondness for gin rummy but to his polished sense of style as well.

 HOSTING A CARD PARTY

A new generation of hosts and hostesses is discovering the fun of these evening diversions, which don't require elaborately set dining tables or multiple courses. All you will need to throw a festive card party is:

- A card table, which can be easily found at most discount stores.

- An attractive card table cover, which is typically made of Ultrasuede, corduroy, or needlepoint. If you want a highly decorative cover, look for a vintage example online; those made decades ago tend to be fanciful.

- A few decks of monogrammed playing cards. Decks from Tiffany & Co. are the gold standard.

- Personalized score pads, available from the Merrimade website.

- Drinks and finger food such as tea sandwiches, pigs in a blanket, or cookies shaped as card suits. The old-fashioned bridge mix is optional.

CHECKERBOARD FLOORS

THERE'S SOMETHING ABOUT A CHECKERBOARD-PATTERNED FLOOR, especially one that is glossy black and white, that calls to mind top hat and tails, marabou-trimmed gowns, and Cole Porter tunes. If it sounds as though I'm describing a Fred Astaire and Ginger Rogers movie, it might be because those rhythmically alternating squares of dark and light tiles make me want to dance—or at least to walk in a staccato fashion.

While black-and-white marble checkerboard floors are considered to be the most classic version, these patterned floors can also be created using square tiles of limestone, ceramic, linoleum, and carpet. The choice of tile color combinations is really limitless, but because checkerboard is such a bold pattern, complementary or tonal pairings seem to work best. By the way, have you ever noticed that checkerboard tile floors are laid either on the diagonal (meaning that the squares look like diamonds when facing them) or in a straight, grid-like manner? The choice is up to you, but diagonally laid tiles do add visual depth to a space, making it seem to go on for eternity.

The late etiquette expert Emily Post, always a stickler for propriety, believed that "the white-paneled wall and black-and-white-marble floor, which are still epidemic among the decorators, are always good style for a small hall or the foyer of an apartment." If a black-and-white

marble floor is an epidemic, then I hope that my own entryway becomes its next victim. Entry halls and foyers are prime real estate for checkerboard floors, where their graphic pattern can welcome guests with a dramatic "Hello!" Also, because such spaces tend to be unencumbered by a lot of furnishings, one doesn't have to worry about the floor's pattern overwhelming a sofa, say, or grandmother's antique Oriental rug. This explains why these harlequin-patterned floors are often avoided in living and dining rooms.

If there is one other room in the house where a checkerboard floor seems equally at home, it's the kitchen. Traditional black-and-white linoleum is one option, although an alternative that is equally as soft underfoot is cork tile, now sold in an array of colors. If your floor is wooden, you might even consider painting it in a checkerboard pattern, something that will add country charm to your kitchen. One final suggestion: if you can't afford to replace the floor in your kitchen or entryway, a checkerboard-painted floorcloth is a terrific option. These painted and treated canvas rugs, sometimes referred to as *oilcloths*, date back to Colonial times. However, there is nothing old-fashioned about the new versions that are made by companies such as Early American Floorcloths and CanvasWorks Floorcloths. In addition to being very durable, they boast all kinds of modern geometric patterns.

SEE ALSO
Painted Ceilings and Floors.

Inspired by a floor designed by famed twentieth-century architect David Adler, this checkerboard floor is different from most because the tiles were laid in slanted fashion, which produces a harlequin pattern.

CHINOISERIE

DID YOU KNOW THAT DURING THE MIDDLE AGES, EUROPEANS believed that China, or Cathay, as the far-away country was then known, was a land of both dragons and men with canine-like faces? It was an outlandish notion, to be sure, but one that helped to fuel the fascinating and enchanting style known as *chinoiserie*. Reaching a high-water mark in the eighteenth century, this popular decorative style was an intoxicating concoction of fantasy and the bizarre mixed with traditional Chinese motifs like tea ceremonies, pagodas, and cormorants. It was a style that, while Asian inspired, was completely a Western invention.

Throughout the seventeenth, eighteenth, and even early nineteenth centuries, the chinoiserie style pervaded the homes of wealthy Europeans in the form of hand-painted wallpapers, fabrics, ceramics and porcelains, furniture, architecture, and garden follies. But it was one house in particular, the Royal Pavilion in Brighton, England, that remains one of the most exuberant examples of chinoiserie. Built in the late eighteenth and early nineteenth centuries by the prince regent (later King George IV), the Royal Pavilion was spared few chinoiserie flourishes. There was the dramatic looking Banqueting Room that was decorated with Chinese-inspired murals, doors outlined in gilt bamboo, and ormolu and gilt dragons adorning sideboards and lamps, not

An interior designer chose Cowtan & Tout's "La Pagode Chine" fabric to lend her powder room chinoiserie flair. A Chinese-style gilt wall shelf and sake cups holding roses were added to heighten the room's sense of fantasy and charm.

SEE ALSO
Bamboo;
Follies;
Valances.

to mention perched atop sweeping curtain valances. Above this scene hung a magnificent chandelier held to the ceiling by a beastly looking, fire-breathing gilt dragon. And to think that this was just one of the many chinoiserie-laden rooms in the palace!

Chinoiserie is one of those decorative styles that never appear déclassé. Its lighthearted fancifulness still lends an element of Oriental fantasy to our homes, though a fantasy whose conjectures are charmingly old-fashioned. Take, for example, chinoiserie-patterned china, still one of the more popular styles of dinnerware today. A plate animated with pagodas and Chinese men in coolie hats introduces sophisticated, imaginative playfulness to your table. And speaking of dining, it's the dining room where you often see walls papered in antique or newly printed chinoiserie wallpaper. Can you imagine a more elegant way to dine than among graceful birds perched in trees or dignified people performing the ritual of serving tea?

When it comes to chinoiserie decorations, the options seem endless. There are blue-and-white Chinese-style urns and vases that look so chic when grouped in great masses, not to mention chairs with Chinese Chippendale backs. You can add little Chinese bells to both ends of your curtain valances or paint a Chinese-inspired umbrella over your room's door. There are stair railings that mimic fretwork, and wallpapers that mimic bamboo, and lanterns that mimic the tops of pagodas. Well, it can never be said that the chinoiserie style is not prolific.

And although you can successfully mix a variety of chinoiserie pieces in one room, please don't lose your head and go overboard, as tempting as it may be. Too much of this style in a room will only turn your home into chop suey, which, by the way, is a mostly American invention, but that's a story for another day.

C | CHINTZ

CHINTZ, THE USUALLY GLAZED AND PRINTED COTTON FABRIC WITH roots in seventeenth-century India, has become one of today's more maligned fabrics. Just mention its name, and many people shudder with thoughts of the bad chintz that was so prevalent in the 1980s. Think tangled prints of bows, ribbons, and flowers that were given overly shiny glazes and that were often forced into ruffles upon ruffles on curtains, pillows, and chairs. Yes, it was cringeworthy, but please don't let this prejudice you against this charming fabric.

Typically strewn with printed flowers, chintz has long enchanted decorators. Ever the design provocateur, Elsie de Wolfe was a great advocate of chintz, touting the fabric's use in city homes in addition to its more traditional country settings. What at first may have startled the smart set later earned de Wolfe the moniker "the chintz lady." Then there were those renegades, Dorothy Draper and Rose Cumming, who took chintz in bold new directions. Draper mixed blowsy cabbage rose chintz with chunky striped walls and saturated color, while Cumming took a more recherché approach, partnering her chintzes (many of which she designed herself) with elegant furniture and sophisticated shades of lilac and mauve. If you like the look of floral chintz but want to avoid any old-fashioned connotations, do as Draper and Cumming

did and partner it with walls painted in vivid hues (a glossy finish would be smart), urbane-looking furniture, and silks and satins. By the way, those floral chintzes with the black backgrounds can be quite chic, a Goth twist to a prim print.

SEE ALSO
*Floral and
Foliage Prints.*

On the other hand, let's take a less city-centric view of chintz and dwell on the pastoral side of its personality. Chintz is a hallmark of the English Country House look, its humble prints a foil for many of those architecturally grand English homes. John Fowler employed chintz in his interiors often, using it to imbue homes with warmth, comfort, and cheer, while later devotees of the English country look Mark Hampton and Mario Buatta also used floral chintzes for a sophisticated country effect, often in city interiors too. In fact, Buatta has been such an adept and enthusiastic patron of chintz that he, like de Wolfe before him, earned the nickname "the prince of chintz." If you ask me, that's high praise.

Whether you take your chintz with a side of cosmopolitan flair like the great lady decorators or if you prefer it in quaint, arcadian settings, chintz is a fabric with great versatility and flair. But don't forget that chintzes come in other varieties. There are glazed geometric print chintzes and striped versions too. And then there is my very favorite chintz of all, a glazed cotton bearing a Venetian blind print. Used often by John Fowler, this chintz was usually made into window shades, ones that were the spitting image of real blinds. Now there is nothing chintzy about that!

A pillow covered in chinoiserie-motif chintz creates a moment of whimsy and animation when placed upon a solid-colored sofa. The chintz's lustrous glazed finish is a nice contrast to the sofa's textured upholstery.

COLLECTIONS

A ROOM FILLED WITH EXQUISITE FABRICS AND FURNISHINGS IS much like Sleeping Beauty. It's beautiful, all right, but it needs to be awakened and brought to life. And few things enliven a room more than a homeowner's collections. Whether one collects books, paintings, art glass, or even Hollywood movie posters, the effect that collections have on a room is immense, imbuing it with warmth and, more important, the homeowner's personality. As Michael Greer once wrote, accessories help to "document the you-ness of you."

Embarking on a collection is really quite easy. The best piece of advice I can give is to ignore what the trend prognosticators are touting as the current must-have accessory and to listen to your instincts. What do you gravitate to when you visit an antiques market or tag sale? What do you like to search for on eBay? Maybe it's Art Deco sterling silver cocktail shakers, or perhaps it's McCoy pottery. Vintage cosmetics ads? Those are quite plentiful, and they look terrific when framed and hung in one's bathroom. The point is that no matter what the "it" is that strikes your fancy, you should indulge your passion for it, current trends be damned!

The more obscure or unusual the collection, the more memorable it is. One of the most lauded tastemakers of the twentieth cen-

A collection of Wedgwood black basalt ware, which was acquired over many years, looks more impressive when displayed together on one table surface, an effect that would be lost if the pieces were scattered throughout the room.

tury, Roderick Cameron, was known for his collection of hands made of materials like glass or wood. The late fashion designer Bill Blass collected lifelike crayfish and crabs that were carved from ivory. Cabaret singer Bobby Short amassed memorabilia that reflected his African American heritage. While each of these collections was unique, their objects all held special meaning for their respective owners.

While the nature of your collection is your choice and yours alone, there are a few guidelines that should be followed when displaying your collections. Collections have impact and look their best when displayed en masse, or altogether. Otherwise, a piece scattered here and there will end up looking like bric-a-brac rather than part of an organized collection. An assortment of antique snuff boxes, for example, would do well to be displayed together on a table surface. And don't forget to edit your collection so that only the choicest pieces are on display. A collector must also be a censor, relegating questionable objects to drawers and closets. It was the late Albert Hadley, the most disciplined of designers, who told his biographer, Adam Lewis, "Building a collection requires a strong constitution and the ability to resist."

 ## CELEBRATED COLLECTIONS

What ties these tastemakers together is a passion for collecting, no matter if they pursued the sublime or the prosaic.

DUKE AND DUCHESS OF WINDSOR: Pugs . . . both living and modeled from porcelain

YVES SAINT LAURENT: Art Deco furniture

DIANA VREELAND: Antique snuff mulls

KENNETH JAY LANE: Orientalist art

ROSE TARLOW: Antique tableware

CAROLYNE ROEHM: Blue and white porcelain

ANDY WARHOL: Cookie jars

DORIS DUKE: Rare orchids

CONVERSATIONAL
CHAIRS

MOST OF US TEND TO PLAY IT SAFE WHEN CHOOSING LARGE, COSTLY pieces of furniture, because who wants to tire of their sofa after a year? That's a smart move, and yet not every piece of furniture in a room needs to be so cautious. When placed in a room's mix, a conversational chair, those chairs with quirky good looks and a unique personality, will not only spark a stimulating dialogue among your room's furnishings but just might also prompt a lively discussion among your guests.

One of the more popular conversational chairs of late is the *loop chair*, made famous in the 1930s by the designer Frances Elkins. If you didn't know that the origins of this chair are nineteenth-century England, you might just think the chair's loopy looks and curvy legs were designed with a Jazz Age flapper in mind. And today the still-produced loop chair looks just as fresh as ever, especially when given a painted finish and a brightly colored upholstered seat.

There is one conversational chair that, despite the fact that it's named for a pest that I loathe, I find to be most appealing: the *spider chair*, designed by (guess who?) Frances Elkins. (Elkins obviously appreciated the value of a conversational chair, considering that she used both the spider and the loop chair in many of her clients' homes.) With sturdy legs reminiscent of the Queen Anne style, an upholstered shield back and seat, and swooping arms, the chair, in a way, resembles a spider. When upholstered in Elkins's preferred choice of leather, the chair's eccentric shape gooses both traditional, well-mannered interiors and contemporary, too-hip-for-thou environments, injecting some welcome playfulness. Look for vintage examples of the spider chair at auction, or seek out reproductions at retail shops like Mecox Gardens.

A laid-back alternative to the spider chair is the now classic *butterfly chair*. Although it reminds me of my first postcollege apartment, the collapsible metal-framed chair with the leather or canvas sling seat has become an icon of twentieth-century design. Best left to modern-looking homes, these chairs never seem to go out of style. While mid-twentieth-century-era butterfly chairs command high prices, newly produced renditions can be found at the big-box stores. My advice is to steer clear of chairs with brightly colored seats and instead choose a neutral color that will prove harmonious with your other furnishings.

There are other charming examples of conversational chairs, including those with backs that look like hot-air balloons, sheaves of wheat (a favorite motif of Coco Chanel), and even musical instruments. No matter which chair you choose, make sure its design has something interesting to say.

Noteworthy for their intriguing and eccentric shapes, the dignified spider chair, the high-spirited loop chair, and the groovy-looking butterfly chair spark interest in rooms where the other furniture is predictable and mundane.

C COQUILLAGE

SHELLS HAVE LONG PLAYED SUPPORTING ROLES IN BOTH ARCHI-
tecture and interior design, often serving as flamboyant accents to
restrained surfaces. The shell motif, known as *coquillage,* even helped
to define one of the most ornate decorative styles of all: rococo. But
coquillage has a secondary, fanciful meaning, that being the adornment
of architectural accents and decorative accessories with shells—and lots
of them.

History provides us with elaborate, if not truly over-the-top, examples of shell-embellished architecture. Take, for instance, Marie Antoinette's shell pavilion at Château de Rambouillet, where practically every
surface—fireplace mantel included—was smothered in shells laid in decorative patterns. The doomed French queen's shell grotto later inspired
a strikingly similar shell-encrusted ballroom in the Neuilly, France,
home of Arturo Lopez-Willshaw, the super-rich Chilean industrialist
and one of the twentieth century's great aesthetes.

For our purposes, though, we might want to take our cue from
something a little less grandiose. In the Bahamas home of the late Lady
Baillie, the famed French decorating firm Maison Jansen designed a
guest room with a mantelpiece and wall paneling that were both festooned with black and white shells. And former magazine editor Marian

McEvoy has garnished her headboard, lampshades, mirrors, and wall plaques with an abundance of shells, all added with the aid of her trusty glue gun.

Creating your own coquillage is not difficult. All that is required is a cache of shells (which, thanks to online shopping, does not require a trip to the beach), the aforementioned glue gun, and a little creativity. Take a large, flat-surfaced picture frame, and to it, glue bleached sand dollars and a border of tiny white seashells. Insert a sheet of mirror, and voilà! A piece worthy of Neptune. Or how about gluing concentric layers of iridescent abalone shells, a particular favorite of the late designer Tony Duquette, to a fiberglass ceiling medallion? Have your electrician install the medallion above a chandelier, where it will serve as a lustrous crown for your light fixture.

A modern way of incorporating coquillage into your décor is with sleek shell wall coverings or tiles. One of last century's more lauded architects, Samuel Marx, often covered walls in flat pearlescent kappa shells as a luxurious backdrop for contemporary furnishings and materials. Achieve a similar look with one of the many capiz wallpapers that are available today. Just remember, though, to balance out the walls' decorative richness with clean-lined furnishings. Otherwise, you'll end up with a case of visual indigestion.

Not all coquillage requires you to pull the glue gun trigger. You can buy shell-laden wall brackets, candlesticks, and obelisks, not to mention lamps, console tables, hinged boxes, and curtain finials. One of my favorite stores that deals almost entirely in coquillage is Christa's South Seashells in West Palm Beach, Florida. Visit the store or the company's website and behold an eclectic array of busts, fountains, sink vanities, and trifles laden in seashells.

CORNER FURNITURE

I DON'T KNOW ABOUT YOU, BUT I FIND A ROOM'S CORNERS TO BE some of the most difficult spots to decorate. Trying to find a piece of furniture that will fit comfortably in a ninety-degree angle can be such a challenge that oftentimes, it's simply easier to leave a corner empty. Rather than neglect those annoying corners, seek out furniture that was made to fit.

The most common example is the corner cabinet. You remember those cabinets with glass-front or open shelves that were typically used in dining rooms to hold a collection of household china? Some might find them old-fashioned, but they don't have to be. While a search at your local antiques stores or on the Internet for corner cabinets will more than likely yield a lot of traditional dark-wood pieces, there are cabinets that are quite dashing and are worth tracking down, including those decorated with snazzy painted finishes, chinoiserie motifs, and mirrors too.

Another option would be to visit one of those unfinished-furniture stores, the kind with the cute names like "Furniture in the Raw." Find an unfinished cabinet whose style is in keeping with your room, and then have it painted in either the room's trim or wall color to look like it is part of the room's architecture. Take note that a corner cabinet is not for dining rooms only. In a living room, display books, collections, or your television in a corner cabinet, or employ one in your bathroom or dressing room for linen or clothing storage.

SEE ALSO
*Banquettes;
Dressing
Rooms;
Occasional
Tables.*

Triangular tables also make excellent corner fillers thanks to their shapes, and they're not as difficult to find as you might think. These typically small occasional tables work well in modestly sized spaces. If you have an empty corner in your foyer, place a triangle-shaped table there and display a potted plant or a piece of sculpture on top. Because hallways have a tendency to be dimly lit, a table lamp positioned on a small corner table will help to brighten the space. And powder rooms can also benefit from such tables, where they can be used to hold gracious essentials like tissues and perfume bottles.

Much like this triangle-shaped table, a piece of furniture that is designed to fit into a room's corner will adequately fill a hard-to-decorate nook while also providing unobtrusive storage or seating.

If you were told to go sit in the corner as a child, it was usually meant as a form of punishment. If only you had had a proper corner chair in which to sit. We've already discussed banquettes that can be built into corners, but there are also chairs that were designed specifically for use in these tight spaces. Most of these chairs have rounded backs for comfort, although some V-shaped chairs do exist. A corner chair, whether it's an antique English walnut version or a modern upholstered wedge, looks so inviting in a home's entryway. It's essential, too, in those homes where guests are requested to sit down and take off their shoes upon entering.

COTTON FABRIC

IS THERE ANY FABRIC THAT EMBODIES THE AMERICAN SPIRIT MORE than cotton? It's a down-to-earth fabric, one that doesn't put on airs. It's sturdy, not delicate. And how many fabrics are comfortable enough to lounge in and upon, appropriate for both clothing and upholstery? As those catchy Cotton Inc. ads say, cotton is "the fabric of our lives."

While democratic cotton has long been a favorite fabric for both town and country, it was Billy Baldwin who helped to elevate the social status of the fabric. Once claiming "My world is entirely cotton," Baldwin boldly used the fabric where, in the past, it had dared not tread: among the rarefied world of Aubusson rugs, FFF (decorator speak for "fine French furniture"), and old master paintings. Baldwin's introduction of cotton to his clients' luxurious interiors meant that many of these stiff, museum-like rooms suddenly became more relaxed and vibrant. Thanks to Baldwin, cotton had conquered Park Avenue.

The beauty of cotton is that you can dress it up or down. If your living room is more of a formal affair, consider glazed cotton for upholstery. The fabric's lustrous sheen will add polish to the space, while at the same time keeping a check on those pieces with the potential for grandiosity. For more casual spaces, a heavy-duty woven cotton or cotton-linen blend, either in a solid color or a print, lends a

SEE ALSO
Chintz.

In an effort to tone down this stool's ornate brassiness, I chose Brunschwig & Fils's "Les Touches" to cover its seat. The print's markings give this cotton fabric a dressy appearance that is in keeping with the stool's polish.

comfortable practicality to sofas, armchairs, and simple curtains, an invitation to kick off one's shoes and relax. Even in those utilitarian rooms like kitchens and bathrooms, cotton's durability and affordability make the fabric a prime choice for shower curtains, tablecloths, and kitchen curtains. I guess you could say there are few rooms where cotton isn't at home.

And just as silks and damasks tend to ratchet up a room's formality and fussiness, cotton serves to tone it down. Cover those antique or gilt chairs in a pretty cotton print. Temper ornate stools and benches with a snappy patterned cotton fabric. Basically, if something seems too "too," then cover it in cotton. It's the great equalizer, making the old look youthful, the fusty become fresh, and the stodgy seem hip. See? Cotton really is the fabric of everybody's lives.

FABRIC HALL OF FAME

Cotton is multitalented, able to coax traditional, ornate patterns into a more relaxing style as well as to enhance contemporary prints' liveliness. Perhaps this dual-nature explains why many of the design world's most revered, and best loved, printed fabrics are made of cotton. They include:

- "La Portugaise" by Brunschwig & Fils
- "La Riviere Enchantee" by Braquenié
- "Old Rose" by Colefax & Fowler
- "Coppelia" by Edmond Petit
- "Chinese Leopard Toile" by Brunschwig & Fils
- "Arbre de Matisse" by China Seas
- "Sabu" by Rose Cumming by Dessin Fournir
- "Hicksonian" by Lee Jofa
- "Spatter" by Hinson & Co.
- "Fazenda Lilly" by Carleton Varney by the Yard

D | DOG PAINTINGS

HAS ANYONE MORE ACCURATELY PEGGED THE PSYCHOLOGY OF THE human-pet relationship than Winston Churchill? Among his many quips was this gem: "Dogs look up to us. Cats look down on us. Pigs treat us as equals." No matter the challenges, we dog and cat lovers tend to have unbridled enthusiasm for our pets, something that often spills over into our homes. How many of us can claim ownership of pillows, trivets, notepads, and Christmas tree ornaments emblazoned with our breed of choice? Quite a few, I'm sure.

An antique print depicting Duchess, an English Springer Spaniel, hangs among shelves of art books. In homes decorated with contemporary furnishings, a black-and-white dog print is often better suited than a traditional oil painting because of its lack of color.

One area of canine collectibles that is a little more highbrow than the rest is that of dog paintings. It was Queen Victoria of England who started the rage for these paintings in the nineteenth century, something that might explain their subsequent appearances in many of the grand English country houses. Here in America, the great designer Mario Buatta, an avid dog lover despite not owning one, helped to make dog paintings de rigueur thanks to his use of them in his cozy English-style interiors. Buatta often hung these dog paintings using satin ribbons and bows, thereby spawning yet another design trend that took America by storm in the 1970s and 1980s.

Someone else who popularized dog paintings was Brooke Astor. According to Albert Hadley, he and Sister Parish included two antique

dog paintings in their overhaul of Astor's Manhattan sitting room. Astor was so taken with these paintings that she bought more, not just to decorate her city sitting room but to line the stairwell of her country home as well. Needless to say, once people heard that Brooke Astor was collecting dog paintings, there was a mad rush to start their own collections too.

While dog paintings have become a hallmark of the English Country House look, certain works—especially those that are more restrained in manner and depiction—can look quite sophisticated in more contemporary dwellings. Not to belabor Billy Baldwin's Manhattan studio apartment (although it is a prime example of how traditional antiques can blend harmoniously with modern elements), but it was here that Baldwin once ceremoniously hung an antique dog painting above his cotton slipcovered sofa and against those iconic chocolate-brown walls. If anything, the painting only enhanced the polish of the other decorative elements.

Whereas dog paintings by British painter Sir Edwin Landseer are some of the most coveted by collectors, there are many examples by other Victorian era and twentieth-century artists that are just as engaging. To see the range of this genre, visit the website of Manhattan's William Secord Gallery, one of the foremost galleries specializing in nineteenth-century dog paintings and drawings. You just might find a painting similar to that owned by Billy Baldwin.

If oil paintings simply aren't your thing, then consider photography. The lauded photographer William Wegman carved out a niche in the art world by photographing his beloved Weimaraners, and dog owners have been commissioning photographs of their pooches ever since. Black-and-white pet photography is particularly appropriate for minimalist interiors where dogs and cats are welcome but where lighthearted or whimsical decorative touches seem at odds with the décor.

D DRESSING ROOMS

A HUNDRED YEARS AGO OR SO, ETIQUETTE DICTATED THAT A boudoir was for sitting, a bedroom for sleeping, and a dressing room for dressing and "making one's toilet," to use the old phrase. In their classic manuals on decorating and the domestic arts, both Edith Wharton and Emily Post spent numerous pages discussing how to properly appoint one's dressing room. Elsie de Wolfe devoted an entire chapter of her tome *The House in Good Taste* to the dressing room and bath, even going so far as to say that "no self-respecting French woman would dream of dressing in her sleeping room."

Although today's private quarters are less regimented, a room devoted to dressing and applying one's makeup is a luxurious convenience. Ideally, your dressing room should be located between your bedroom and bathroom, although a dressing room can really be carved out of any space. Seldom-used home gyms, guest rooms, and rooms lacking a specific purpose are all candidates for a dressing room makeover.

When it comes to your dressing room's décor, you really should make it as feminine, glamorous, or opulent as you want. There is no need for you to literally go broke, however, when decorating this personal space. Built-in shelving and drawers are certainly nice to have, but if they're beyond your budget, try the following. Around the perim-

eter of your dressing room, place inexpensive shelving units, cabinets, and rolling wardrobe racks (easily found at stores like IKEA or the Container Store). Then, taking your cue from the late fashionista Nan Kempner's Manhattan dressing room, hide everything behind walls of curtains. Attach curtain rods along the room's walls, and then hang premade curtain panels or even attractive bedsheets from them.

SEE ALSO
Ballroom Chairs; Skirted Tables.

A vanity is a must for a dressing room. A vintage mirrored dressing table replete with crystal-knobbed drawers is very Jean Harlow, while a kidney-shaped, fabric-skirted vanity calls to mind Sandra Dee. If you have a small desk or side table that has seen better days, simply skirt the table in fabric and buy a piece of cut glass to protect the surface. Makeup seems easier to apply when seated, so place a small stool or chair in front of your vanity. As I mentioned earlier, a delicate ballroom chair makes a fine vanity chair. On your dressing table, you will need to have good lighting (perhaps a pair of small matching crystal lamps working in tandem with a close-by floor lamp), a mirror, decorative glasses to hold cosmetic brushes, and small trays in which to store cosmetics or jewelry. Oh, and don't forget a pretty perfume bottle or two.

As de Wolfe also quipped, "Know the worst before you go out!" If you do have built-in closets in your room, clad their door fronts in mirror; it's both sparkling and practical. Or simply hang a full-length mirror on the back of the room's door. Finally, if your room's size will allow it, add a daybed, a chaise, or a small settee. That way, you can relax among all of your lovely finery and plan your outfit for the next day.

A dressing room should make you feel like a glamour puss. Seen here is a vintage mirrored dressing table, a small tufted stool, feminine fabrics, and a crystal lamp, all of which create a luxurious atmosphere in which to dress and apply makeup.

D DUST JACKETS

BOOKS MAY GIVE THEIR READERS PLEASURE, BUT THEY ALSO present us with design challenges. Should we organize our books by spine color or by title? Should we display them horizontally? Vertically? And what do we do about those dust jackets?

To me, a bookshelf full of arresting dust-jacketed books is a beautiful sight to behold, but some people find it to be a distraction that can mar an otherwise tranquil room. If that's you, the best solution is to either shed books of their dust jackets (make sure to keep them in a safe place) or shroud their covers in paper or vellum.

The great designer Nancy Lancaster once covered the books of her London library in red paper, something that added dramatic impact to the room's shelves. Legendary designer Thomas Britt wraps his books and periodicals in glossy cream-colored paper with handwritten labels on the spine that help to identify the underlying hardbacks. Because Britt's living room is decorated in tones of cream, beige, and soft browns (including its bleached boiserie walls), creating a soothing oasis of cream-colored books makes a lot of sense.

If you decide to cover up the books on your shelves, there are many decorative papers from which you can choose. Although it can be expensive, Italian marbled paper will give your tomes an antique look,

Book dust jackets, especially those from the early to mid-twentieth century, are often masterpieces in their own right. Here, Cecil Beaton's Ballet *(the dust jacket was illustrated by the author himself) is displayed facing forward to allow enjoyment of its cover art.*

much like the marbled end boards of old books. There are luxurious papers that resemble crocodile skin, leather, and even wood grain. Or you can take the economical yet still chic approach and simply sheath your books in kraft paper.

On the other hand, many of us prefer to treat a dust jacket as an integral part of a book's value, believing that it should remain partnered to the book with which it came. Dust jackets not only protect books but can be works of art too. Some peo-

ple collect books with dust jackets and pages that were illustrated by artists like Cecil Beaton, Rex Whistler, Osbert Lancaster, and Edward Gorey. Others gravitate to dust jackets that bear a certain pattern such as malachite prints or sunbursts, both of which I like to collect.

In fact, if you have books with particularly striking or clever dust jackets, you might want to place them facing forward on a shelf so that the jacket's front cover is displayed prominently. London-based designer Richard Adams uses dust jackets to add wit to his apartment, placing such books as *Snobs* and *Unsuitable Company* at the ends of his glass-sided bookshelf so that the visible titles will foster some laughter. You could do something similar by placing books with catchy titles on top of cocktail tables or stacks of books. Titles like *The Working Girl Must Eat* or *Live Alone and Like It* might add levity to your décor. (That is, of course, if you have a sense of humor about such things.)

 EVENING ROOMS

BECAUSE OF THAT PESKY LITTLE THING CALLED WORK, MANY OF US don't have the luxury of enjoying our homes during daylight hours. It's usually after 6 p.m. when we can fully appreciate the fruits of our design labors, often while relaxing after a hard day's work or entertaining friends and family. If most of our time spent at home is in the evening, doesn't it make sense to decorate a room that will look its best at night?

Evening rooms are designed to soothe frayed nerves and provide snug refuges from the outside world, a task that makes them prime candidates for cozy dark colors. Walls painted in deep shades of brown, blue, red, and even green are ideal, especially when they are given a semi- or high-gloss finish. Flat finishes have a tendency to suck the light—and life—out of a dark-colored room, while a glossy sheen will help to reflect light and create a nice warm glow. If you're especially daring, you might want to consider coloring your evening room black, which is not as depressing a color as it might seem. Cecil Beaton's swank London drawing room had walls covered in black velvet with gold and silver embroidery reflecting glints of light. If those walls could talk, I'm sure they'd have something witty, if perhaps quite naughty, to say.

It goes without saying that lighting is most important at night. Forgo the overhead lights, as they tend to emit an antiseptic glare that is about

What's my ideal evening room? It would have to include
cozy colors, a comfy chair, a reading lamp,
and Alfie, my Cavalier King Charles Spaniel.

EVENING ROOMS ARE DESIGNED TO SOOTHE
FRAYED NERVES AND PROVIDE SNUG REFUGES
FROM THE OUTSIDE WORLD.

as inviting as a hospital ward. More attractive by far is a combination of table and floor lamps as well as sconces, all of which will bathe the space in warm, flattering light. Pink incandescent lightbulbs or lampshades lined with pink fabric will not only enhance your evening room's appearance but will also give your face a nice rosy glow. Remember that lamps are not your only friends when it comes to lighting a room. Materials like brass, gilt, and chrome act like light amplifiers thanks to their reflective surfaces, so a smattering of furniture and accessories in these finishes will impart additional glimmer to this environment.

Most important of all, though, is that your evening sanctuary be filled with comfortable furniture. This is not the place for ladder-back chairs or hard little antique settees. Roomy upholstered sofas and armchairs are a tonic for weary bodies just as tufted stools and ottomans are for tired feet. Whichever furniture you choose, make sure to cover it in a fabric that is soft to the touch, yet durable too. Brushed cotton, velvet, corduroy, and certain wool fabrics are invitations for nocturnal lounging. Silks are rather stand-offish and don't do well with people eating and drinking on them, something that really should be encouraged in an evening room.

The finishing touches to your evening room? Pleasant music, a mystery novel, a roaring fire, a full-bodied Cabernet or a single-malt Scotch, and someone to relax with, especially if it's your dog or cat.

 EXOTIC PRINTS

DECORATING WITH A GLOBAL PERSPECTIVE HAS BEEN EN VOGUE
for hundreds of years. If you remember that day in history class when the
East India companies were discussed, you know that textiles from India
and China, for example, were exported like crazy in the seventeenth
and eighteenth centuries to a European continent that was desirous of
the new and exotic. Foreign-made fabrics depicting faraway landscapes
and peculiar motifs of trees and flowers lent international flair to formal European interiors. Interestingly enough, neither time nor commercial air travel dampened enthusiasm for these textiles. Designers of
the 1960s and 1970s were equally as mad for exotic patterns, lavishing
rooms in yard upon yard of ikats and paisley prints that were fitting for
the Age of Aquarius. Still today, these global fabrics remain a popular
choice for injecting worldly sophistication into one's home.

Asia has provided us with all kinds of exotic prints, too many to
mention in just one entry. There is the now classic Tree of Life motif,
introduced to the European market in the seventeenth century. Now a
staple in most interior fabric lines, those elegant arborous prints made
by such fabric houses as Braquenié, Pierre Frey, and Schumacher lend
themselves to sophisticated, well-appointed interiors. For those of you
with a more Bohemian slant, seek out affordable Tree of Life cotton

bedspreads, plentiful on the Internet, for use as bed coverings, of course, but also as wall hangings, curtains, and tablecloths.

Ikat prints of Central Asian origin are popular once again thanks to their bold, bright colors and graphic, abstract patterns that work well in a variety of interiors. Whether rendered on silk or cotton, ikat prints impart youth and colorful vigor to a room. Ikats are not meek, so balance out their use with solid-colored fabrics. And did you know that the paisley print was not born in the Scottish Highlands? That kidney-shaped print is really of Persian ancestry, though it also found popularity in Asia too. Paisley fabrics in muted, somber colors skew traditional, while those in eye-popping tones read more modern. One of my favorite early-1970s interiors is a living room whose walls were covered entirely in brightly colored paisley and floral Indian bedspreads. Decorated by Mica Ertegun and Chessy Rayner of MAC II, this interior remains fresh and exciting looking even today, a testament to the timeless appeal of exotics.

And we can't forget Africa, where kuba cloth, that wonderful woven fabric with the geometric designs, has long been valued not only by those who live on that continent but by foreign sophisticates too. Because of kuba cloth's rough-hewn texture and neutral tones, it works especially well in contemporary homes where bright color is not an option.

If you're looking for guidance on how best to adapt exotic prints for traditional interiors, look no further than British designers Robert Kime and John Stefanidis. Kime's revered textile line is rife with exotic prints, including those adapted from old Algerian, Turkish, and Indian patterns, and mostly rendered in easy-to-live-with colors. And Stefanidis's equally attractive fabric line includes exotics that are more stylized and contemporary looking. So you see, there is an exotic print for everyone, whether you're a globe trekker or an armchair traveler.

Ikat prints partner well with each other because of their strongly similar patterns. On this French settee, three different fabrics, all of which bear shades of pink, red, blue, and yellow, offer far-flung exoticism to an otherwise traditional furnishing.

FAUX BOIS

IT CAN BE SAID OF MANY OF US THAT WE CAN'T SEE THE FOREST for the trees. Well, how are we supposed to when trees are so interesting to look at? In fact, trees, their bark, and their inherent wood grain have captivated people as far back as the Bronze Age, when artisans sometimes decorated pottery to resemble wood. Thousands of years later, faux wood grain finishes were painted on walls, doors, and furniture as fanciful embellishments that added decorative flair. Although this imitation of wood was used throughout Europe and as far away as China, it was the French who christened this decorative style with the charming sobriquet *faux bois*.

A garden bench such as the one in this illustration might look like it is shrouded in a tangle of tree branches, but in reality its concrete frame is designed to emulate them. A fern print cushion bolsters this imitation of nature.

Interpreted as "false wood," faux bois comes in many forms. There is china, painted to mimic wood grain. Some of the most coveted of all faux bois porcelain china is that made by Meissen centuries ago, although if you prefer something more casual and less fragile, there is good-looking wood grain dinnerware being produced today. Fabric and wallpaper also come bearing a wood

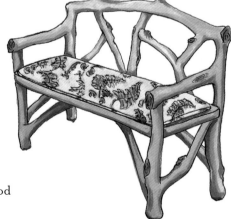

TREES, THEIR BARK, AND THEIR INHERENT WOOD
GRAIN HAVE CAPTIVATED PEOPLE AS FAR BACK
AS THE BRONZE AGE.

grain design, but rather than implying woodland whimsy, they impart a sophisticated, organic look to the furniture and walls that they adorn. Both Nobilis and Martha Stewart Living make faux bois print wallpapers that are really quite striking, with Martha Stewart's version catering to those with tight budgets.

In fact, Martha Stewart clearly has a fancy for faux bois. Visit her website and you'll see lessons on how to paint your furniture with a faux bois finish, carve a pumpkin in a faux bois pattern, and decorate your cupcakes in chocolate wood grain. And Stewart also collects early twentieth-century concrete faux bois furniture, a highly sought after subgenre of this decorative style. With wood grain or bark texture etched into their concrete frames and branch-like legs and arms, these sturdy tables and chairs are resilient on the patio, where they help to make that segue between the inside of a home and the outdoors.

I do think there is a distinction between faux bois that is appropriate for city dwellings and that for country homes. For town, faux bois fabrics in silk and velvet and branch-like furniture in metals or slick faux finishes work best. Out in the country, think down to earth: cotton, linen, carved wood, and concrete. If, however, you want to concoct a Black Forest fantasy in your high-rise apartment or a silvery, sleek birch forest in your country pile, then I see no reason why you shouldn't do so.

FAUX FINISHES

MORE OFTEN THAN NOT, IMITATIONS TEND TO BE MERE SHADOWS of the real thing. Take imitation vanilla extract, for example, or pleather. Horrors! Faux finishes, however, are one type of imitation that, if executed well, not only capture the essence of the original but can look even better than the real thing.

Faux finishes are decorative treatments, usually rendered in paint, plaster, or paper, that are applied to the surfaces of walls, ceilings, floors, trim, furniture, and decorative accessories. The twist is that these finishes are meant to look like something that they're really not, and in many cases, it's difficult to tell that they're not authentic. Some of the most classic types of faux finishes are those that mimic minerals or stones, especially marble. A room with marble walls and trim does look ravishing, but you would have to be as rich as Croesus to afford such a luxury. But walls or molding painted to look like marble? Well, that's an economy that has more pizzazz than the real deal, something evidently not lost on the Duke and Duchess of Windsor. The walls in their Paris entry hall had *faux marbre* (or faux marble) painted walls. And if you look through any books on English Country House style, you'll often find great halls whose walls or baseboards have the very same treatment, an appropriate choice for a house in the country.

In an effort to transform my apartment's fake fireplace from ugly duckling to swan, I hired a friend to paint the wooden mantel in a blue tortoiseshell faux finish and to mirror the fireplace's surround and hearthstone.

SEE ALSO
Chintz.

that bear artistic or graphic interpretations of flowers and leaves, imparting a modern sensibility to a traditional genre. Some of the most colorful, if not eye-popping, flowers were those designed by Austrian-born designer Josef Frank. Still produced and still in demand today, these midcentury prints captured buds of blue and leaves of hot pink or orange—flowers as Mother Nature never intended. Then there are the colorful floral fabrics of the late Madame Paule Marrot. Championed by Billy Baldwin as well as Jacqueline Kennedy (who used Marrot's Les Tulipes fabric in her bedroom at the White House), Marrot created bold prints of brushstroke-like flowers and leaves. Her plucky and gamine prints are also still in production today, available through Brunschwig & Fils.

But we mustn't discuss flora and foliage to the exclusion of the men (or those women with masculine aesthetics), who are better off forgoing the sweet, romantic flowers in favor of earthier prints. If you're all about wood tones, brass, and antique oil paintings, then you just might be a good candidate for the tried-and-true prints of the late English textile designer William Morris. Rendered in the Arts and Crafts style, Morris's flowers and leaves are stylized in a natural kind of way.

D. Porthault's "Trèfles" print features stylized clovers trailing on a cornflower-blue background. When used as a table skirt in a sunny room, the fabric serves as a delightful spot upon which a potted violet, a basket holding a fern, and Constance Spry's classic books on flower arranging sit pretty.

❧ | BELOVED BLOSSOMS

Overcome any ambivalence about floral prints by seeking out fabric or wallpaper that portrays your favorite flower, which might possibly be the same as one of these famous flower-lovers:

- **LOUIS XIV:** Sunflower
- **CHRISTIAN DIOR:** Lily of the Valley
- **PAULINE DE ROTHSCHILD:** Lilies and White Lilacs
- **DUCHESS OF WINDSOR:** White Lilies and Orchids
- **EMPRESS EUGENIE:** Violets
- **CLARE BOOTH LUCE:** Night Blooming Cereus
- **MADAME DE POMPADOUR:** Hyacinth
- **CECIL BEATON:** White Orchid
- **DAVID HICKS:** Tuberose

F | FLOWER ARRANGEMENTS

"FLOWERS MUST BE THOUGHT OF AS 'GRAVY,'" A SENTIMENT PURportedly uttered by that glamorous 1930s British decorator Syrie Maugham. While it's true that flowers aren't the meat of a room's décor, a bouquet here and there certainly adds a lot of flavor to one's home. I would even go so far as to say that flowers imbue a space with as much warmth and vitality as flattering lighting, comfortable fabrics, family pets, and, yes, people!

Trends in floral arrangements change as often as women's hemlines and heel heights. Look at interior photos taken in the 1930s, and you'll often see striking, not to mention sculptural-looking, arrangements of both trumpet and calla lilies, always in shades of white. Fashionable ladies of this era gravitated to white flowers, and perhaps none more so than the Duchess of Windsor, who picked white flowers to the exclusion of other colors. Perhaps the popularity of white flowers was a result of that other popular 1930s fad, the all-white room, made famous by Syrie Maugham. What's interesting to note is that it was another member of the 1930s London smart set, the late floral designer Constance Spry, whose impact on how we view flowers is still felt today. Spry took a then revolutionary approach to cut flowers, thinking of them as part of a room's overall décor. And she also upended the definition of a proper floral arrangement, inserting grasses, kale, and seed pods, for example, alongside traditional flowers. The results were arrangements that were natural in look and bohemian in spirit. They took London, and America too, by storm.

The easiest type of arrangement to assemble is that which involves only one type of flower in a single color. Buy a large bunch of coral-colored roses or blood-red carnations (carnations seem to last forever!) and place them en masse in a silver julep cup, a glass beaker, or some other decorative container. However, keeping in mind Spry's admonition that flowers should jibe with one's décor, make sure that the color you choose is complementary to your room's color scheme. No clashing colors, please.

There is not a single room in one's home where flowers aren't a welcome addition. Waking up to a small posy of flowers on one's bedside table can help to ameliorate that annoying buzzing of the alarm clock. Place a few hospitable-looking flowers next to the sink in one's powder room. Fragrant flowers go a long way to combat stale house smells too. Note, though, that in rooms like entry halls or spacious living rooms, a large vase or urn holding something tall has the most impact. For these spaces, try statuesque flowering branches (depending on the season, quince and forsythia are two options) or simply branches of good old greenery. Dorothy Draper was known to fill vases with rhododendron leaves, while I like to clip Magnolia branches for display in Chinese urns. To me, there is nothing prettier than a Magnolia's glossy bottle-green leaves, ones that are made even glossier with a rubbing of cooking spray applied with a paper towel.

Some of the easiest floral arrangements to assemble are those that feature either one type of flower or a mixture of varieties in solo or tonal colors. Urns, decorative boxes, and even drinking glasses can be commandeered for vases.

F | FOLLIES

FOR MANY SEVENTEENTH- AND EIGHTEENTH-CENTURY EUROPEAN aristocrats, no manor was complete without a garden folly or two. Ideally situated in a natural pastoral setting, garden follies, which are buildings and pavilions whose sole purpose is to amuse, were used by their owners as bucolic retreats and places for entertainment. And for many of these aristocrats, the more outrageously designed the folly was, the better. During that European folly-building frenzy, all kinds of whimsical follies were built, including those that resembled underwater grottos, Chinese teahouses, and even a giant pineapple.

Based upon a folly at Désert de Ritz garden in Chambourcy, France, this ornate-looking example is meant to imitate a Tartar tent, which refers to those tents used centuries ago by the nomadic Tartar tribe.

Although the rage for these conceits may have abated during the nineteenth century, there were a fashionable few who continued to be enchanted by these architectural flights of fancy. One of the twentieth century's most notable tastemakers, Charles de Beistegui, built a bevy of follies at his famed French country house, Château de Groussay. His follies included a metal structure painted to resemble a Tartar tent, a Palladian bridge, and a pyra-

SEE ALSO
Chinoiserie;
Faux Finishes.

mid. One of the more recent follies to garner attention was that built by designer Bunny Williams. Her folly-like pool pavilion, situated on Williams's Connecticut property, resembles a Greek temple, one made of wood. The structure's columns are made of oak tree trunks, while the pediment is encrusted in pinecones. Nature never looked so good.

If you own a large expanse of land, consider it a canvas upon which to scatter a folly or two. A fanciful wooden bridge built over a creek or stream can be considered a folly, especially if its design resembles a Japanese bridge, for example. Or what about a Russian fantasy of a gazebo, one topped with a brightly colored onion dome roof? On a smaller scale, you could give Fido his own folly, a doghouse that looks like a pagoda or a diminutive medieval-style castle.

Follies don't have to be built from scratch or confined to exteriors only. Try transforming a tool or gardening shed into a folly, something that isn't so difficult to do because of a shed's typically small size. Perhaps you love all things chinoiserie. Why not paper the interior walls of your shed with Chinese bird wallpaper, hang some Chinese paper lanterns, and assemble a few pieces of Chinese Chippendale-style furniture? Now you've got your very own Chinese teahouse, one in which you can relax, read, entertain, and yes, even take tea.

Many of us have empty rooms in our house that look so forlorn, just waiting to be given a purpose. With a little imagination, that room could be made into something akin to a folly. Paper its walls in tortoiseshell paper (both Cole & Son and Schumacher carry versions), and paint the crown molding in a matching faux finish. Add a sofa covered in russet-colored velvet, a lacquered black Parsons table, and a pair of glazed claret ceramic lamps by designer Christopher Spitzmiller, and your room will feel like the inside of a very glamorous tortoiseshell box.

G | GARDEN STOOLS

HOW MANY PIECES OF FURNITURE CAN BOAST THEIR USEFULNESS both outdoors and indoors, in wet and dry conditions, and as a stool and a table? For such a decorative-looking item, the garden stool, or garden seat as it is sometimes called, is quite the workhorse. Its durable glazed-ceramic composition gives the stool sturdiness to brave outdoor elements like rain and wind, not to mention the ability to withstand the pressures of weighty backsides when perched upon them.

The version with which you may be familiar is the classic Chinese drum-shaped stool, its design dating back a thousand years. Often glazed in a solid color or adorned with blue-and-white Chinese motifs, the garden drum stool is like the little black dress: appropriate in any setting. But in keeping with the stool's decorative intention, whimsical versions also abound, depicting elephants, frogs, or turtles, as well as examples made of stacked ceramic cushions and even stacked ceramic pumpkins. On my own outdoor balcony, I have an Italian garden stool that looks like a giant bunch of asparagus—something that might have appealed to the garden-loving Nancy Lancaster's droll sense of humor.

Garden stools may have been conceived for use in gardens, but they really prove their versatility inside the house. In the living room, try positioning one next to an armchair, where it can serve as a small

FOR SUCH A DECORATIVE-LOOKING ITEM,
THE GARDEN STOOL, OR GARDEN SEAT AS IT IS
SOMETIMES CALLED, IS QUITE THE WORKHORSE.

table, one to hold drinks, books, and any other essential-for-relaxation items. Designer Miles Redd often peppers his interiors with glamorous silver-glazed drum stools for just this very purpose. Keep one at the ready next to a fireplace, perhaps stacked with books, or stow a pair of them underneath a console table. At your next cocktail party or soirée, bring the stool into the center of the action and allow it to mingle with the guests, one of whom will inevitably plop down on it.

For most furniture, bathrooms are not their friends; all of that moisture and steam can wreak havoc on their appearance. Not so for the garden stool that is made to resist water's more negative effects. If you like to luxuriate in a bath with a good book and a glass of wine, a stool placed at arm's length can be pressed into service as a tub-side table. Have you ever noticed that many newly built walk-in showers don't have wall recesses to hold shampoos and soap? A remedy is to put a ceramic stool in your shower corner (preferably away from the stream of water) to hold your soap dish and other necessities. And not to be indelicate, but if you're tired of having to contort your body while standing to shave your legs, a garden-cum-shower seat will make life—and shaving—much easier.

A ceramic garden stool, which is decorated with traditional blue-and-white Chinese motifs, is today typically found indoors where it serves as both a handy occasional table and a spare seat.

G GARNITURES

IF YOU HAVE EVER SEEN A PHOTO OF A FORMALLY DECORATED living room from the early to mid-twentieth century, chances are the room's fireplace mantel was furbished with what is known as a *garniture.* Owing its name to the French word *garnir,* meaning "to garnish," a garniture is a matching set of decorative accessories that was intended to be displayed together, usually on top of a mantel. Often, you'll see antique garnitures that consist of identically patterned porcelain vases and urns, while other examples might include an ornate clock and coordinating candlesticks. Historically, garnitures were composed of three, five, and occasionally seven pieces due to the notion that an odd-numbered assemblage was more aesthetically pleasing than a symmetrical, even-numbered set.

Historically, garnitures were odd-numbered sets of like-minded decorations, such as porcelain, that were typically displayed on fireplace mantels. Still, today, they lend flair to the surfaces that they embellish.

Today, many people view garnitures as vestiges of old-fashioned decorating, a formal relic of the period-style rooms that were once in vogue. (Up until the latter part of the twentieth century, it was not uncommon to find rooms that were devoted entirely to

one decorative style, like Louis XV or early American.) And indeed, unless your home is formally attired, a traditional garniture might look out of place. However, most fireplace mantels can still benefit from the uncluttered cohesiveness that a garniture provides. Make a garniture modern by creating your own grouping of like-minded accessories that brings a pulled-together yet casual look to your fireplace.

SEE ALSO *Brackets.*

Keep in mind that when objects are displayed together, they need to be visually harmonious in scale, finish, and theme. Otherwise, things will look off-kilter. For guidance on how to create our own garnitures, we should look to the English decorator John Fowler, whose carefully assembled groupings sometimes consisted of clocks, pairs of candelabra or vases, and sculptures. The key to his garnitures' success was to partner objects of similar height, scale, and style and display them in odd-numbered groupings.

The most effective way to decorate your mantel would be to start with a pair of items, perhaps two small, matching lamps or a pair of glass hurricanes, and place one at each end of your mantel as anchors. Then position one object, like a ceramic urn or cachepot, at the mantel's center to impart a sense of symmetry to the fireplace wall. If you prefer a looser, more tousled look, keep the pair of anchors in place and add three unique yet similar objects between them. Artwork, shells, foo dogs, and obelisks are all attractive options for mantel displays. Just make sure to balance your garniture along the entire length of the mantel so that one end doesn't get the lion's share of the objects.

Finally, who is to say that antique garnitures must be displayed only atop fireplaces? You could arrange the set on wall brackets to give maximum decorative flair to an otherwise empty wall. Garnitures can also be used to help banish the unsightly gap that often exists between short cabinets or shelving and a room's ceiling. Congregating the entire garniture on top will add much-desired decorative height.

GEOMETRIC PRINTS

DESPITE THEIR MODERN, AND AT TIMES MOD, APPEARANCES, GEO-
metric prints have been around since ancient times, having been
used to decorate textiles, pottery, and furniture. (Could their ancient
popularity have been because their straightforward lines were easy to
draw with such limited tools?) Even nineteenth-century wallpaper was
sometimes produced in surprisingly contemporary-looking designs of
stripes, diamonds, dots, and zigzags. Looking at these historical papers,
one can be forgiven for thinking that they had been designed a century
later for an Albert Hadley project!

Because of their crisp, orderly patterns, geometric prints add
emphasis to whatever they decorate, much like an exclamation point
does at the end of a sentence. The question that you have to ask yourself, though, is how loudly you want your furnishings to exclaim "Look
at me!" Take those assertive yet still appealing prints associated with
the late David Hicks. Designed by Hicks during the groovy 1960s and
1970s, these brazen diamonds, hexagons, and chevrons did have a tendency to beat one over the head with their boldness, though not in an
unpleasant way. Because we now live in tamer times, the best way to
decorate with these confident geometric prints (which are still popular
with designers and homeowners alike) is to take a balanced approach.

*Used here
for curtains,
Victoria Hagan's
Platinum Ring
fabric has gusto
because of its
bold circles and
squares, and
yet it is easy to
live with, too,
because of its
subtle neutral
tones.*

BECAUSE OF THEIR CRISP, ORDERLY PATTERNS, GEOMETRIC PRINTS ADD EMPHASIS TO WHATEVER THEY DECORATE, MUCH LIKE AN EXCLAMATION POINT DOES AT THE END OF A SENTENCE.

Carpet your living room floor in a Hicksian pattern, but tone it down with solid-colored upholstery. Or splash a traditional antique chair in Hicks's La Fiorentina or Clinch patterned fabrics, for example. The chair's old-fashioned propriety will help to keep the fabric's audacious pattern in check, while the fabric's energetic print will eradicate any of the chair's dourness. You see? It's the yin and the yang.

On the other hand, there are some (myself included) who prefer the subtlety of small geometric prints in soft hues. These prints, which are of a smaller scale than those of Hicks, were favored by the great decorating duo Sister Parish and Albert Hadley. In their interiors, geometric prints were used alongside Parish's beloved rag rugs, wicker furniture, and decoupage as well as Hadley's preferred Parsons tables, contemporary art, and mirrored cornices. These geometric-flecked fabrics and wall coverings always looked terrific, imparting an American kick that kept the Parish-Hadley mix looking fresh and not too serious.

The reason why Parish and Hadley's prints are still so easy to live with today is because of their neutral backgrounds and disciplined markings. Some of my favorites? Sister Parish's Tucker, Burmese, and Bolero and Albert Hadley's modern-inflected Astor Stripe and Trixie, a star-and-dot print that I liked so much, I papered both the walls and ceiling of my study in it. These geometric prints are most certainly not in your face, partnering easily with an array of patterns and furnishings. Rather than shout for attention, these prints merely beckon you to take notice.

SEE ALSO
Parsons Tables.

 GROTTO FURNITURE

THE LATE DUARTE PINTO COELHO, A PORTUGUESE-BORN DECORA-
tor whose impeccable interiors were revered the world over, once said,
"Fantasy is the most important ingredient in decorating." If this is true,
then few accents add more flavor to a room than grotto furniture.

Artificial grottos date back to ancient Greece and Rome, where
shrines to water goddesses were built first in caverns and later as tem-
ples. By the eighteenth century, grottos were fashioned as free-standing
follies, often lavished with shells and rocks to imply watery caves. These
grotto follies were especially popular in England, where a number of
decorative grottos still stand today. Just as beguiling is grotto furniture,
which typically features stylized representations of shells, dolphins, and
Neptune's trident. Some of the most charming examples of grotto furniture are chairs, benches, and stools that resemble large scallop shells.
Traditionally, this shell seating was made of wood that was painted in a
silvery, iridescent finish. However, for those whose decorative tenden-
cies were less flamboyant, dark polished-wood grotto chairs were made.

Grotto furniture found its way into the homes of style maver-
icks with an eye for the unusual. The prominent Art Deco artist and
designer Erté once fashioned a conchological fantasy room in a client's
French château. With its theme of water, the room was decorated with

SEE ALSO
*Coquillage;
Dressing
Rooms; Follies.*

shell-encrusted mirrors, commodes, and a grandfather clock, among which sat three silvery grotto chairs and a table. Helena Rubinstein, once again the design trail blazer, used grotto chairs in her Manhattan dining room. Even in a Mark Hampton–decorated room, one conceived as a paean to the great classical architect Sir John Soane, there stood a shimmery grotto chair, an unconventional accent among straight-laced classical artifacts.

What makes grotto furniture so appealing is that it's a far cry from your run-of-the-mill pieces. Grotto furniture adds a whiff of eccentricity to a space, a quirky yet chic touch that will help to differentiate your home from that of everybody else. If you come across an antique wooden grotto chair, especially one with an iridescent finish, buy it on the spot. The chair will make a most glamorous vanity chair, making you feel like Venus on the half-shell as you apply your makeup. If you're not feeling so Poseidon adventurous, perhaps a less exuberant mahogany grotto stool placed in your study or living room is preferable.

While antique grotto chairs can be difficult to source, there are two twentieth-century adaptations that are readily found both online and at antiques shops. The first variation, one made famous by French designer André Groult during the 1920s and 1930s, is a wooden chair with a carved shell back. Less expressive in style and scale than traditional grotto chairs, these more restrained versions make for elegant hall or dining chairs. A later twentieth-century take on the grotto chair was designed specifically for the patio. Made of aluminum, these outdoor chairs have reticulated shell backs and curvy legs embellished with a fish scale–like pattern. Their whimsical design makes these chairs a worthy partner of the boldly patterned outdoor fabrics that are so popular today. These chairs wouldn't, however, look out of place if you brought them indoors, especially in beach houses, where a plentiful use of them accentuates the coastal locations of these homes.

Upholstered in sturdy outdoor fabric, two vintage aluminum grotto chairs provide out-of-the-ordinary seating on my high-rise balcony.

HOUSE STATIONERY

THANK HEAVENS THAT STATIONERY IS ONE OF THOSE NICETIES
that still have traction in today's electronically driven world. While
most of us are familiar with social stationery (think notecards and call-
ing cards), you may not be aware that your house should be outfitted
with its own stationery, something that I like to call "house stationery."
A house attired with a few choice pieces of writing paper will not only
run more smoothly but will also be more hospitable and amenable to
entertaining too.

 The most basic type of stationery to collect is notepads—and plenty
of them too. Custom-printed notepads showing your full name,
your initials, or your house's name (there's no reason why your home
shouldn't have one) are an affordable luxury, especially considering that
you'll want to keep one in every room of the house for those times when
you need to make a list, jot down a phone number, or capture a bril-
liant idea that inevitably comes to you in the middle of the night. Two
popular stationery lines, Dempsey & Carroll and Mrs. John L. Strong,
sell elegant house tablets whose imprinted covers feature gold pineapples, Eiffel Towers, and even butlers. I have to say, though, that my
all-time favorite notepads were those used by the late designer Albert
Hadley. Who can forget his trademark white paper pads with the big

*"Easy
entertaining"
means having
a ready supply
of blank menu
and place cards,
a menu book,
and fill-in
invitations
like these from
Tiffany & Co.
Handwritten
invitations
are gracious
alternatives to
e-mails.*

collection of interior paintings hangs in her home's library. Bill Blass was also a fan of room paintings, although he also sought out antique architectural drawings as well.

At the moment, some of the most collectible interior paintings are those done by the late artist Walter Gay and the painter Jeremiah Goodman, whose renderings include the homes of Greta Garbo, Betsy Bloomingdale, and Bill Blass. It was Gay who was responsible for those wonderful depictions of Elsie de Wolfe's beloved Versailles estate, Villa Trianon. Other notable interior illustrators include James Steinmeyer as well as the late Alexandre Serebriakoff and decorator Mark Hampton. Hampton's charming watercolors of iconic interiors can be seen in his classic book on design history, *Legendary Decorators of the Twentieth Century*.

Perhaps you should consider commissioning portraits of your own rooms. Although an illustration might seem superfluous when you can simply take a photo of your favorite space, that photo will not delight you the way a painting can. Hire a professional artist or a very talented friend to capture your favorite room using oils, watercolors, pastels, charcoals, or whatever medium pleases you. If you're lucky enough to call British designer Nicky Haslam a close friend, by all means ask him to illustrate your room's rendering. Haslam's paintings are some of the most beguiling that I've seen!

If all else fails, you can always create your own interior illustration, whether you can paint or not. Find a photo of a room that holds special meaning to you—say, your childhood home's living room—scan it into your computer, and use photo software to transform your photo into a brushstroke painting. Print it onto heavy stock paper, and then have it professionally framed so that it can hang in your home as a reminder of happy times. However, if you're particularly fond of a room in your current house, don't hesitate to immortalize it on paper and then display the illustration in the very room that inspired it.

A framed vintage interior rendering, perhaps drawn decades ago by a designer or architect, is displayed against bookshelves filled with design books. Interior illustrations are highly sought after by designers and design enthusiasts alike.

J | JIB DOORS

AT FIRST GLANCE, A JIB DOOR MIGHT SEEM AN ARCHITECTURAL novelty, but more than a glance is needed to know that a jib door even exists. A door that lies flush with a wall, a jib door lacks surrounding molding, prominent hardware, and other architectural features that often distinguish traditional doors. It is often treated to the same finish as the walls around it so that it remains undetected.

The purpose of a jib door is to give a wall a seamless appearance. Let's say you choose to cover your dining room's walls in a beautiful chinoiserie wallpaper, one decorated with flowering trees and flitting songbirds. Wouldn't it be a shame to disrupt the bucolic scene with a framed wooden door leading to the kitchen? The solution would be to install a jib door whose surface can be papered just as the wall, allowing for an uninterrupted scene. You won't even know the door is there.

Small spaces like entryways, hallways, and powder rooms are prime candidates for a jib door because a regular door might appear too conspicuous in such a tight space. The late Albert Hadley made good use of the jib door in his Manhattan apartment, where his hallway walls were covered in a dramatic lacquered-red corrugated type of paper. Rather than allow a standard door to lessen the decorative impact, he installed a jib door, one sheathed in the very same wallpaper, leading to the guest

A jib door, with its baseboard and painted finish mimicking the surrounding walls, conceals this entry hall's coat closet. An antique barometer was hung from the door to give the impression of continuous wall space, while only a small knob indicates the presence of a door.

bathroom. When the door was closed, any hint of there being a bathroom beyond it was eliminated.

The thing to keep in mind about jib doors is that their hardware is not like that of a regular door. Hinges can't show or they will blow the jib door's cover, so the use of concealed hinges (which are easy to find at good hardware stores) is essential. How do you open a jib door? Usually with a jib door pull, one that barely protrudes beyond the door because of its attachment to the door's interior edge. Specialty hardware manufacturers like E. R. Butler & Co. and Nanz, both located in New York City, carry these pulls.

It's important to note that jib doors have graced some of the most lauded and influential interiors in design history. Remember the famous Horst photograph of Pauline de Rothschild peeking into her bedroom with its antique Chinese-papered walls? De Rothschild was peering through a jib door that was also covered in the same paper, although her door did have a door handle attached to it. John Fowler also used this architectural device in many of his interiors, especially those with papered walls. One of the more elaborate jib doors I've seen was created by David Hicks. In a hallway, he papered a jib door with marbled wallpaper like that on the surrounding walls, while a baseboard was added to the door's bottom to mimic the rest of the space. The most inspired touch, though, had to be the wooden vitrine that was attached to the door so that it moved as one with the door. Unless someone told me a jib door was there, I might have missed it. Then again, that's the whole point.

K KLISMOS CHAIRS

THE LATE BRITISH-BORN DESIGNER T. H. ROBSJOHN-GIBBINGS once wrote that the klismos chair was "perhaps the most beautiful chair ever made in the world." That was certainly high praise coming from an avowed modernist, especially considering that the klismos chair can trace its roots back to ancient Greece.

With its slender saber legs, the klismos chair is gazelle-like in its leggy sleekness. But it's the chair's curved back, one that ancient Greek furni-

ture makers adapted to echo the shape of the human back, that makes this chair a remarkable example of early ergonomic design.

While the classic version of this classical chair is made of a wooden frame, there are revamped klismos chairs made of acrylic or metal, good choices for those who prefer sleek finishes. Keep in mind that these elegant little chairs deserve equally elegant fabrics. Leather, creamy velvets, and subtly patterned silks are worthy choices

One of the oldest prototypes in design history, the classical klismos chair remains popular today because of its simple yet stately design and, more important, its comfortable, curved back.

A LEOPARD-PRINT CARPET'S TYPICALLY NEUTRAL HUES PROVIDE A SURPRISINGLY SUBTLE FOUNDATION FOR A ROOM'S FURNISHINGS.

While you can cover an entire floor in leopard print and it will look chic, covering an entire room in leopard print textiles usually doesn't work. Leopard print fabric is a different beast from its carpet counterpart, best used only in small doses. Try peppering a sofa with a leopard print throw pillow or two, preferably in a luxurious fabric like velvet or silk, or covering a small ottoman or stool in that signature tan with black spots. If you wish to be daring, upholster a sofa in a traditional leopard print fabric, but make sure that your room's other furnishings look tame. Or try a leopard print fabric that is less Serengeti, more Palm Beach. These updated versions of the leopard print tend to come in cheerful, bright colors like blue or pink, making them appropriate for family rooms, little girls' rooms, and any other space where décor needs to be punchy, not racy.

It might seem counter-intuitive, but leopard-print carpet behaves much like a solid-colored carpet. The sprinkling of small spots tends to blend together when viewed from a distance, while its neutral markings make it easy to decorate with.

There are a few notable leopard print devotees who got it right. In one of her infamous "Why Don't You . . . ?" columns for *Harper's Bazaar,* Diana Vreeland suggested using fake leopard skin on one's bathroom floor. French writer Jean Cocteau's study, decorated by Madeleine Castaing, had leopard print walls. (Despite what I said earlier about using leopard print in moderation, this exuberant use of leopard print seemed to work in the writer's home. Then again, Cocteau was also one of the few people who managed to pull off an unruly hairstyle best described as "standing on end.") And then there was the designer Tony Duquette. To paraphrase the old nursery rhyme: when he was good with leopard, he was very, very good, but when he was bad (as when he covered an entire toilet in leopard print silk), he was horrid!

 LINEN CLOSETS

IN A PERFECT WORLD, WE WOULD ALL OWN LINEN BY D. PORTHAULT, Pratesi, Frette, and Léron as well as a big closet in which to store it. No matter where your linen hails from, a sliver of a closet or a chest devoted solely to the storage of your linen is really a handy thing to have.

First, let's address the décor of your linen closet. A little effort without a lot of expense is all that is required to create a closet that is worthy of your linens. Many of us have leftover rolls of wallpaper lurking around our homes that can be hung in our linen closets. If you don't have extra paper lying around, it's not necessary for you to go to the expense of buying some when an affordable can of paint will suffice. Also, take into consideration your closet's shelves, especially since your linen will be resting on them. One option would be to cover your shelves in a sturdy yet soft fabric. Cotton and felt are two budget-conscious fabrics that come to mind. Or you could use a decorative self-adhesive shelf paper, one adorned with stripes, geometric prints, or Greek keys, for example. If you choose to keep your shelves bare, at least consider gluing a decorative ribbon along the front edge of the shelves, something that will lend a bit of panache.

Storing your linens properly is not only good for them but it will also make your life a little easier. Hang laundered tablecloths on hang-

Keeping your linen chests or closets organized is easy if you tie each set of table linen with decorative ribbon—just like a pretty package. A small sachet filled with mildly fragrant potpourri keeps confined spaces smelling fresh without leaving its scent on napkins and mats.

SEE ALSO
Faux Finishes.

chite room? That's easy thanks to the wallpaper firm Cole & Son; their popular malachite print wall covering was conceived by the late Italian designer Piero Fornasetti, whose surrealist-like furnishings often featured the malachite motif. Then there's the malachite faux finish, a classic treatment for wooden tables and boxes. However, larger pieces can certainly be lavished in the same manner. Crown molding, doors, cabinetry, or four-poster beds painted to resemble malachite will look costly but won't require spending all of your rubles.

Of all the uses of malachite, though, it's on the dining table where the mineral motif is really a feast for the eyes. Many in-the-know collectors have malachite print dinnerware in their china cabinets. Christian Dior and Neiman Marcus produced versions of this patterned china, both of which are worth seeking out on china replacement websites. You can even swathe your table in malachite print tablecloths, napkins, mats, and flatware. The finishing touch to your Russian-inflected table? Why, borscht and beef stroganoff, of course!

A collection of exotic-looking malachite objects—some made of real malachite and others painted to imitate it— plays a starring role on this side table. Grouped together, the colorful collection has more drama and impact.

MR. MALACHITE

Of all the legendary designers, Tony Duquette (1914–1999) is probably the one most associated with malachite. In his often-photographed homes, malachite's swirling pattern effusively appeared on pillows, walls, tablecloths, plates, bed skirts, and bed canopies. Add to that Duquette's elegant furniture and opulent-looking accents, and the result could have been too rich. And yet it wasn't, thanks to Duquette's quirky creativity and American ingenuity. Much of the designer's décor was really pastiche, cobbled together from cardboard, egg cartons, pipe cleaner, bird feathers, and Styrofoam. The effect was dazzling, one which those Russian tsars would have found beguiling.

M | MIRRORED SPACES

A ROOM SURROUNDED BY MIRRORED WALLS IS A SIGHT TO BEHOLD
. . . and behold . . . and behold, thanks to the multitude of reflections
bouncing all over the place. Banish any notions of carnival fun house
from your mind though. A mirrored space is really quite chic, a gleaming counterpoint to a home's more formal, restrained rooms.

To quote Billy Baldwin, "Hallways are meant for mirrors," a sentiment that must have been shared by Louis XIV, whose Hall of Mirrors
at Versailles still ranks as one of the most glittering of all spaces. A less
grandiose but still regal-looking hall of mirrors was the apartment entryway of the great songwriter and wit Cole Porter at the Waldorf Towers
in Manhattan. Decorated by Baldwin, the entry hall's walls and ceiling
were entirely sheathed in mirror, appropriate considering that Porter
once wrote a song titled "Mirror, Mirror." Those of us with postage
stamp–size entry halls and foyers might do well to follow suit. Not only
will the mirrored walls trick you into thinking that the space is much
larger than it really is but they will also provide you with a place in which
to do some last-minute primping before heading out into the world.

To understand how effective mirror is in making cramped spaces
look roomy, consider those average-size (that is, small) Manhattan
apartments where mirror is frequently used to stretch the truth. Some

*Mirrored walls
blur the line
between the
reality of a
room's narrow
size and the
fantasy of a
vast space.
When placed
in entry halls,
mirrors also act
as glamorous
amuses-bouches
that whet
one's appetite
for what lies
throughout the
rest of the house.*

MIRRORED WALLS WILL TRICK YOU INTO THINKING
THAT A SPACE IS MUCH LARGER THAN IT REALLY
IS WHILE ALSO PROVIDING A PLACE TO DO SOME
LAST-MINUTE PRIMPING.

apartment dwellers will choose to mirror the wall behind their living room sofas and end tables, while others will use it on the room's fireplace wall and chimney breast, typically located opposite one's sofa. And sometimes, you'll see both walls covered in it, providing the room with dueling reflections as well as seemingly increased proportions. No matter which wall (or walls) of your living room you deem mirror-worthy, consider covering them in large squares of antiqued mirror (mirror that has been treated to look old and cloudy) that are held together at each corner with gilt rosettes. (Think of a rosette as a large, fluted nail head.) This is the way the French have done it for centuries, and as we can see with Versailles, they really have a way with mirrors.

Bathrooms, powder rooms, and dressing rooms can't seem to function without mirrors. In these spaces, mirrors serve to tell us if we have spinach between our front teeth, a cowlick in our hair, or crow's-feet around our eyes. Perhaps this isn't the most ringing endorsement of mirror, but it does have its positive attributes too. When used floor to ceiling in a bath or dressing room, mirror helps to brighten the space, a boon in rooms where natural sunlight is often lacking. And there's no denying that a mirrored bathroom exudes glamour, a befitting backdrop for your prettiest potions and lotions, not to mention that marabou-trimmed dressing gown. As Dorothy Draper once said, "The more mirror-minded you become, the more your house will reflect a shining charm."

SEE ALSO
Dressing Rooms.

 MONOGRAMS

THERE ARE SOME WHO THINK THAT MONOGRAMMING ONE'S HOUSE-hold effects is equivalent to a dog marking its territory. I happen to disagree with that, but then again, I'm Southern, and heaven knows that Southerners love to emblazon everything, sometimes even toilet paper, with their initials. But just like chocolate, liquor, and trashy novels, monograms are best enjoyed in moderation.

Table, bed, and bath linen are the perfect canvas upon which to have one's initials or cypher—a fancy name for a monogram—embroidered. Choose an embroidery thread color to match the linen for a discreet monogram, or go with a bold or contrasting color for a look that is catchy, not to mention casual looking too. Don't monogram every bit of table linen that you own, however, as that will only look showy. As a cautionary tale of fanatical monogramming, simply look through the Sotheby's catalog for the Duke and Duchess of Windsor auction. Practically every tablecloth, bedsheet, bath mat, handkerchief, and handbag bore Wallis's cypher, three interlocking W's that were often topped with a small crown. Even her bedroom windows had pediments with carved and painted W's on them. Of course, Wallis was Southern, but in defense of my region, I think her roots only partially account for her overzealous monogramming.

Architecture is another opportunity for monograms. One of Europe's great twentieth-century decorators, Emilio Terry, once crafted a gorgeous circular entryway floor for a Paris apartment. It was made of radiating bands of alternating light and dark wood, with its central medallion bearing the homeowners' initials. In one Madeleine Castaing–designed interior, there was a fireplace hearthstone that had the initials of the mistress of the house etched into it. If you're worried about the permanency of this type of house tattooing, then look for a needlepoint, hooked, or stitched rug that bears your first or last initial as a way to personalize your floors. These types of rugs are easy to find online, and the beauty of them is that you can take them with you should you ever move.

Furniture shouldn't be ignored when it comes to monogramming. Once again, Emilio Terry figures into this discussion, as he was responsible for designing a hall chair with an engraved "C.B." (the initials of his client Charles de Beistegui) on the chair back. Albert Hadley also had a wood chair with his initials appearing on its back. (The chair was an antique, so it was certainly a fortuitous find.) A tastefully painted monogram on a chair might be easier to achieve than a monogram carved by woodworking.

There are a million other items that can bear your mark. Dining chair slipcovers look smashing when made of plain linen or cotton that has been embroidered with a scripted monogram. And let's not forget silver barware, silver flatware, dinner china, crystal, tissue box covers, to-go beverage cups, and other sundry bits and pieces. But heed the late protocol maven Letitia Baldrige's advice when it comes to monogramming one's linen (although I think it should pertain to silver too): "Monogram with your maiden name, so you'll get all the monogrammed bed linens in the divorce."

Once used by a designer's grandmother as a "telephone" chair, this family heirloom was treated to a lavish embroidered monogram, which reflects the chair's fanciful shape and sentimental value. The chair's blue–and–white ticking provides subtle context for the monogram.

M | MURALS

OVER THE YEARS, MURALS HAVE GRACED THE WALLS OF SOME VERY swish places like Bemelmans Bar, located at the Carlyle Hotel in Manhattan. Its mural, one that portrays fanciful scenes of Central Park, was painted by none other than Ludwig Bemelmans, creator of that little French schoolgirl Madeleine. (Can you imagine a more charming place in which to quaff Kir Royales?) Across the hall, in the Café Carlyle, are musically themed murals painted by the noted French costume designer and artist Marcel Vertès. In fact, Vertès must have had a knack for mural painting, having been commissioned by Elsie de Wolfe to paint the library ceiling in her beloved Versailles home, Villa Trianon. And it was Tony Duquette, a protégé of de Wolfe, and his painter wife, Beegle, who were responsible for the charming, naïve murals in their famous home, Dawnridge in Beverly Hills. If there were ever six degrees of separation, I'd say this was it.

Murals are first and foremost a form of decorative embellishment, an artistic way to enliven one's walls with scenes that really should have meaning to the homeowner. But did you know that murals are painted opportunities for escapism too? A wall bearing a rendering of the old family homestead will take you on a sentimental journey back to your family's roots, while a lively view of the Eiffel Tower has the ability

My sister painted this mural of a trompe l'oeil niche of shelves within my living room's real, built-in niche. The painting depicts some of my favorite things, including shells, books, and a bust of my design idol, Albert Hadley.

your home solely with furnishings that half of North America also owns. But mix in a few pieces of needlepoint that you created with your very own hands, and you have now introduced the essence of you into your home. Perhaps it's a pillow that depicts your favorite pair of Manolos, or maybe it's a set of coasters with landmarks of your favorite cities.

If you don't want to take up needlepoint but like the look of it, search eBay or Etsy for canvases that somebody else stitched. These can be used to cover chair seats or pillows or wrapped around bricks for use as doorstops. And you know those small square drinks tables from IKEA that everybody owns? Place a piece of vintage needlework on top of the table (taping any unfinished edges underneath the needlework), and then cover it with a piece of glass in the matching size.

Personality aside, needlepoint also brings something very important to a room: texture. A space with only one kind of fabric will look a little flat. But add a needlepoint rug to the floor or a pillow to one's sofa, and the embroidery will add depth. One clever idea with which I am taken is to duplicate the pattern of your favorite printed fabric onto a needlepoint pillow. Simply take a swatch of the fabric to your local needlepoint shop, and have them find somebody to paint the pattern onto a canvas for you. You can even hire people to do the stitching too. Your favorite fabric is now unique décor.

I admit that if there is one downside to working in needlepoint, it is that cloyingly sweet designs abound. Ignore them in favor of geometric prints that, when stitched, have a graphic look that goes with any type of décor. And sophisticated motifs like Greek keys, Aegean scrolls, and Chinese pagodas will also keep your needlepoint current with the times. But remember to temper your enthusiasm when taking needle to thread and avoid a too-prodigious output. As that acerbic Michael Greer once wrote about needlepoint, "There should never be so much that it suggests the output of a dedicated convent."

 **OCCASIONAL TABLES**

HAVE YOU EVER BEEN TO A FRIEND'S HOUSE FOR COCKTAILS, ONLY to find yourself seated in a chair, drink in hand, and with no nearby table upon which to rest your glass? If only your host had thought to place an occasional table close by, you might not have been forced to hold your drink the entire night, the warmth of your hands quickly taking the chill off your martini.

One of the more offbeat versions of the occasional table, this slender corkscrew table is tall enough to stand alongside an upholstered chair or sofa, allowing for effortless placement of a drink or book.

Usually positioned next to a chair or sofa where it can hold a drink, a small lamp, or perhaps a pair of eyeglasses, an occasional table heeds the decorating commandment that calls for some sort of table to be located within reach of all seating in a room. Although by definition occasional tables include end tables as well coffee tables, the most versatile are those that are slender and lightweight, easily moved to spots where they can be of most use.

While the range of occasional table styles is vast, a survey of the most famous examples would have to include the Adjustable Table E1027, the rather clinical name for the sublime tubular steel and glass circular table that was designed by Eileen Gray in

SEE ALSO
*Garden
Stools.*

1927. Part of the permanent collection at the Museum of Modern Art (MoMA) in New York, Gray's still-stylish table is available today at the MoMA Store as well as at Design Within Reach. This seems a good time, by the way, to mention that a contemporary-looking occasional table is an easy way to update a traditional interior. Its small size provides a suggestion of modernity while still being palatable to even the most dyed-in-the-wool traditionalists.

Occasional tables don't have to be bona fide tables either. You can create an erudite-looking table by stacking your favorite design books one on top of the other and placing them next to a chair or bed. The bonus to this option is that it takes some of the pressure off of those overburdened bookshelves that couldn't possibly accommodate another book. And as mentioned earlier, garden stools make for handy occasional tables, though they are best used near chairs of low to moderate height. After all, to be most effective, these tables need to be of comparable height to the seating they accommodate so that they can truly rise to the occasion.

 FOREVER STYLISH OCCASIONAL TABLES

The occasional table's small size encourages designers to lavish it in comely shapes and alluring finishes that appear too sumptuous when used on larger furnishings. Think of these tables as small, satisfying indulgences.

TINI TABLES BY OOMPH: These spindly-legged drinks tables, available in an array of bright colors, are known for their fabric-covered tops.

THE ALBERT TABLE BY LIZ O'BRIEN EDITIONS: A simple square table made fabulous thanks to its high-gloss, fabric-wrapped finish.

THE HALMA MAN TABLE BY SOANE BRITAIN: Reminiscent of a chess pawn, this round table comes in wood, cast bronze, resin, or rattan.

NADINE CHAIRSIDE TABLE BY ALEXA HAMPTON FOR HICKORY CHAIR: Resting on curvy legs, this square wooden table adds shapeliness to a room.

ORANGERIES

ORANGERIES, ENCLOSED STRUCTURES DESIGNED TO SHELTER ORANGE trees and other tender vegetation during winter, might seem superfluous to the modern home, but in seventeenth-century Europe, they were hardly folly. An indispensable way to protect one's investment in those rare and expensive fruit trees, orangeries were admittedly architectural indulgences too; at times owners ornately disguised their practical purposes. Perhaps not surprising, one of the more beautiful and grand orangeries is that at Versailles, which can still be visited today.

Although the fad for orangeries eventually waned, the idea of an indoor garden space remained a popular one, with winter gardens being all the rage in Victorian-era homes. Simply a sunny indoor room designed to house plants and sunlight-starved people, winter gardens have remained in favor among many garden-loving aesthetes. Take couturier Christian Dior, for example, whose oft-photographed winter garden, located in his Paris home, included a floral and bird print fabric that covered the walls and, fittingly, potted palms. Another great designer, Valentino, boasts a chinoiserie-themed garden within his French château, one replete with sumptuous banquettes, Chinese-style garden stools, Chinese wallpaper panels, and, like Dior, those potted palms.

Today, whether loosely referred to as an "orangery" or a "winter garden," a room filled with potted trees and plants as well as comfortable furniture allows you to enjoy the fruits of the outdoors from the comfort of your home. If you're lucky enough to have one room that you can devote to such a purpose, then consider decorating your orangery with furnishings that echo the outdoors, like floral and botanical print fabrics, wicker or rattan furniture, and big round planters holding, for instance, lemon trees. However, if you can't commandeer an entire room for your winter garden, try carving out space within an existing room. Large sunny windows are ideal spots for a table filled to the groaning point with cachepots and pots of plants, while bay windows seem made for small-scale orangeries, especially when filled with tall potted citrus trees or a settee surrounded by blooming plants.

And going back to where we started, it's the orange tree that remains one of the most fashionable horticultural accessories of all, so much so that the pots in which they are housed tend to be equally as magnificent as the trees themselves. Fashion designer Hubert de Givenchy (just like Louis XIV long before him) has simple yet seriously chic silver tubs in which his orange trees live during their wintertime indoor retreat. Another option are those large blue-and-white Chinese fish bowls, usually perched upon an Oriental-style wooden stand, that can hold small orange trees, palms, or any number of other petite trees. With such attractive furnishings, how can your orange trees, not to mention your orangery, not thrive?

SEE ALSO
*Banquettes;
Cachepots;
Chinoiserie;
Floral and
Foliage Prints;
Garden Stools.*

Even seven floors above ground, this high-rise sunroom looks like an outdoor patio. An earthy driftwood table holds potted plants and Sam Houston the cat, while a metal nest of crafted eggs, a branch candelabrum, and a mirror reminiscent of shells emphasize the space's garden-like atmosphere.

P | PAINTED CEILINGS AND FLOORS

CONSIDERING THAT CEILINGS AND FLOORS ARE TWO OF THE MORE prominent features of a room, it's surprising that many of us treat these surfaces to little more than a predictable coat of white paint or, in the case of floors, brown wood stain. A decoratively painted ceiling, one that depicts a scene, for example, or even an imaginative color choice, adds an element of surprise to a room discovered upon looking upward. Perhaps just as unexpected are painted wooden floors, which are always on solid footing, decoratively speaking, especially when they possess great charm and flair.

Dorothy Draper once wrote that ceilings "can do almost as much for your room as a sunny or cloudy sky can do for the landscape under it." That is an apropos comparison considering that ceilings have long been painted to mimic the sky, whether as a realistic representation of puffy clouds against a blue background or simply a coat or two of azure-colored paint to suggest the sky overhead. Pale-blue ceilings are still popular today due in part to the transcendent effect they have on rooms (a blue ceiling can *almost* make you feel as though your room is open to the elements), not to mention that this cool shade pairs well with a host of wall colors, including gray, khaki, aubergine, moss green, and creamy white. For an effect that is truly heavenly, you could take inspi-

A parquetry pattern, which is painted in shades of yellow, bestows flair on an otherwise plain wooden floor. By selecting strongly similar rather than highly contrasting colors, the room's designers avoided a floor that clashed with its surroundings.

SEE ALSO
*Checkerboard
Floors; Faux
Finishes;
Stencils.*

ration from the ceiling at Grand Central Station in New York, famously painted with constellations.

Rather than embarking on a major renovation to remedy ceilings that may be too low or too high for a room , consider employing color instead. Some bright colors can have a smothering effect when applied to low ceilings, but they can do wonders in bringing high ceilings down to scale. On the other hand, light, neutral shades can have an uplifting effect on a room, visually adding feet to your room's height. And if you wish that your ceilings would simply disappear, borrow this trick from Albert Hadley: paint your ceiling black as he did in his Manhattan apartment. Rather than caving in on a room's occupants, a black ceiling magically seems to vanish.

Earlier I discussed how one can paint wood floors to imitate black-and-white checkerboard or treat them with a faux marble painted finish, but did you know that with a flick of your paintbrush, you can create modern-looking spatter-painted floors that resemble those popular with our Colonial American ancestors? Of more recent vintage are those fabulous star motif floors, often made of wood or marble inlay, that famed early twentieth-century architect David Adler had installed in quite a few chicer-than-chic houses. Such floors would be frightfully expensive to commission today, but a star painted smack dab in the middle of your room's floor—easy to achieve with the use of a stencil— would look scintillating. And if Elsie de Wolfe can paint an old map on a ceiling as she once did, there's no reason why you can't paint a compass on your floor, one that indicates your home's navigational direction.

The cleverest of all painted floors, though, has to be those in the Manhattan home of socialite and philanthropist Bunny Mellon. Her floors have painted shadows on them so that no matter the weather outside, the sun seems to always shine indoors.

P PAINTED FURNITURE

PAINTED FURNITURE, WITH ITS BRUSH-WORKED DECORATIVE scenes or ornamentation, has long been prized by collectors for its inimitable good looks and élan, qualities that still make it highly valued today. Some of the most alluring antique examples are those by Italian artisans who, often forced to work with mediocre-quality native woods, typically masked their furniture's inferior composition with richly painted finishes rendered in mostly upbeat colors. Whether it depicted fanciful scenes or it was garnished entirely in decorative motifs, Italian painted furniture displays a flair for the dramatic, appropriate for the country that gave us opera.

Although decorative painting might have ceded ground last century to painted faux finishes or—horrors—no finish at all, such painted furniture still possesses great charm, one that has a cheery effect on today's interiors. A bureau painted with traditional landscape scenes in miniature, for example, provides an amusing counterpoint to a room's more serious-minded furnishings, cajoling the room into a more relaxed mood. Painted furniture can also be helpful in unifying a room's decorative scheme. Let's say your bedroom resembles a lady's garden with walls and fabrics strewn with patterns of flower bouquets. A somber-looking, dark-wood dresser would only interrupt the decorative effect,

PAINTED FURNITURE STILL POSSESSES GREAT
CHARM, ONE THAT HAS A CHEERY EFFECT ON
TODAY'S INTERIORS.

SEE ALSO
*Faux Finishes;
Stencils.*

a jarring moment in an otherwise continuous floral fantasy. Not so with a gaily painted dresser, especially one festooned with small flowers or boxwood garlands.

The other attribute of painted furniture is one that is now more important than ever. In an era when so many furnishings seem very much the same, a hand-painted decorative finish transforms a piece into something completely singular, a break from the monotony of mass production. That coffee table that you bought online, which all of your friends also own? Why not add personality to it with the aid of a paintbrush? Paint some motifs on the tabletop (perhaps a Greek key border or a scattering of fleurs-de-lis). If you're really talented with a brush, paint a scene reminiscent of Michelangelo or Matisse. If freehand painting isn't your thing, consider using a stencil to help guide you.

And don't overlook antiques shops, where painted furniture seems to abound, probably cast off by owners who regrettably failed to appreciate what makes decoratively painted furniture so special. Often affordable, this furniture is rich in uniqueness, a one-of-a-kind way to set your home apart from the mundane.

The owner of this desk happens to be a talented decorative artist. He painted the desk's surface in a faux marble finish and added a cup of coffee, a pair of scissors, blue-and-white plates, and envelopes to further embellish this charming painted piece.

P | PANELED WALLS

OF ALL OF THE WAYS TO ENRICH A ROOM'S WALLS, PANELING LOOKS the richest. Traditionally, wall paneling, usually made of carved wood, was applied to large expanses of wall space to help to warm up a room (literally, in those pre–central heating days) as well as to enliven the space in an orderly fashion. It was in eighteenth-century France, no surprise, where paneling reached ornate heights, intricately carved and crafted into what became known as *boiserie*.

Come the late nineteenth century, paneled rooms became a hallmark of aspirational decorating, adorning the homes of robber barons, railroad magnates, and the superwealthy. For American Anglophiles, wood-paneled walls in the tailored English style could often be found in studies, libraries, and other rooms where propriety and coziness were in order. Francophiles preferred the rococo richness of boiserie in their living rooms, drawing rooms, and dining rooms. While some of these paneled rooms were American made, the most coveted paneling was the antique variety imported from England or the Continent.

Although paneling, both old and newly milled, is quite costly, don't discard the idea of a paneled room, because there are numerous ways to duplicate the effect without the expense. In keeping with Elsie de Wolfe's thought that "the most beautiful wall is the plain and dignified painted wall, broken into graceful panels by the use of narrow moldings," you can affix wood or plaster molding to your walls in large panes that mimic traditional wood paneling. This type of faux paneling can help to bring any far-reaching walls down to size, creating a more comfortable, intimate space.

In lieu of molding, wallpaper borders or ribbon trim can be glued directly to walls. Under the watchful eye of the former first lady Jacqueline Kennedy, the French design firm Maison Jansen decorated the White House Treaty Room, covering its walls in green flocked wallpaper and adding red patterned paper borders in a paneled fashion. The result was reminiscent of sumptuous paneling. Or you could simply take a paintbrush to your walls, creating realistic-looking paneling in the trompe l'oeil style or rendering a graphic interpretation with painted blocks of color.

One more thing to consider if you mock-panel your walls with molding is whether to embellish the wall space inside the panels. Upholstering the wall within its paneled confines will add noise-absorbing softness to the space, whereas printed wallpaper will punctuate your walls with panes of pattern. You can even insert antiqued mirror inside large panels to impart sparkle within your paneled room. The possibilities of paneling are endless.

By painting real or implied paneling in shades of the same color, the decorative effect is subtle yet still significant.

SEE ALSO
Passementerie;
Trompe L'oeil;
Wallpaper
Borders.

P | PARSONS TABLES

FEW CLASSROOM PROJECTS HAVE LIKELY PRODUCED WORK AS stylish and enduring as that of the Parsons table. As the story goes, French designer Jean-Michel Frank, while lecturing at the Parsons School of Design's Paris branch sometime in the 1930s, summoned students to design a supremely simple table that would remain stylistically absolute in a range of surface finishes. The collaboration between lecturer and students eventually resulted in a table that, in a way, resembles an angular, upside-down U, with both its squared-off legs and top having comparable thicknesses. And thus the Parsons table was born, notable for its "Why didn't I think of that?" simplicity.

The Parsons table's unadulterated design allows it to mingle comfortably with both traditional and contemporary furnishings. A small bench holding books fills the ample space beneath this table.

Just as Frank had hoped, the Parsons table remains essentially the same table no matter the finish. There are wooden Parsons tables with luxurious marquetry finishes as well as the rough-hewn-looking cerused, or limed, finish. Mirror, plastic laminate, lacquered paint, fabric, and

THE PARSONS TABLE IS NOTABLE FOR ITS "WHY DIDN'T I THINK OF THAT?" SIMPLICITY.

leather are also commonly found on the surfaces of the Parsons table, as is wrapped cane, a finish of which Billy Baldwin was particularly fond. In fact, these wrapped cane Parsons tables, often fitted with glass tops, are still produced by Bielecky Brothers, Inc., in New York and are considered by many to be the height of American chic.

SEE ALSO
Wood Finishes.

When square shaped, the Parsons table can be employed as a sofa side table, small cocktail table, or snappy dining table. The rectangular versions are more conducive for use as console tables (they look great when placed behind sofas), desks, or library tables. But it's their markedly simple profile that gives them such versatility, striking a classic note when surrounded by contemporary furnishings or a modern one when ensconced among antiques. In fact, there are few interiors that wouldn't benefit from a Parsons table, unless, of course, you live in a museum of period pieces.

Although those Parsons tables finished in luxurious materials can be quite pricey, there are plenty of thrifty options available at stores like West Elm and IKEA, whose version of the Parsons table, the Lack table, has become a design favorite. No matter what you pay for your Parsons table, though, think of it as a worthwhile investment that will pay off stylish dividends for years to come.

P | PASSEMENTERIE

DO YOU REMEMBER THE FAMOUS SCENE IN *GONE WITH THE WIND* in which a desperate Scarlett, planning to visit a jailed Rhett Butler in hopes of convincing him to loan her money, has Mammy whip up a dress using old green velvet curtains with yellow braided cording and tassels? Those braiding and tassels, technically known as passementerie, transformed what could have been a plain velvet dress into a frock fit for a lady, one that turned the heads of both Rhett and those Yankee prison guards. (It's too bad that after all of that effort, Rhett didn't have a dime to loan to Scarlett!)

Resembling a brooch, a velvet-and-silk rosette was applied to each side of a slipper chair's scrolled back. Think of rosettes and other passementerie as jewelry for your curtains and upholstered furniture.

Just like Scarlett's dress, curtains and draperies often need passementerie to look gussied up. A flat ribbon tape attached along the edges of a tailored curtain panel looks polite and neat, while trim embellished with little pom-poms or jeweled crystals, for example, is best reserved for fancier curtains made of dressy fabrics. Traditional curtains are often cinched at their middles with braided and tasseled tiebacks, a type of passementerie that acts like a curtain's belt, allowing it to be hitched to an anchor that is attached to the wall. Some passementerie tiebacks are so resplendent, made of such materials as metal, acrylic, wood, feathers, or precious stones, that it's awfully tempting to wear one on your body as a necklace or a waist sash.

SEE ALSO
Slipper Chairs.

Upholstered chairs and sofas are also opportunities for passementerie. Bullion fringe, that trim with the row of long, sometimes multicolored braids, looks rich when used in lieu of a tailored fabric skirt. Because bullion fringe is opulent, it's best partnered with luxurious fabrics like silks and velvets. However, if you prefer fabric skirts along the bottoms of your seating, then try embellishing the skirt's bottom edge with a ribbon tape or trim, or save this ornamentation for use on sofa cushions and throw pillows.

Of all passementerie, my very favorite has to be the rosette, which perhaps is best described as a round adornment, much like a brooch, that is embroidered with delicate silk braiding. One designer I know enhanced a pair of scroll-back slipper chairs with rosettes placed on each side of their curved backs, while another designer added a charming rosette to the center of a rarely used but pretty nonetheless small silk chair cushion.

Tired of your plain lampshades? Passementerie can be applied to edges of lampshades to give a custom look to an off-the-shelf shade. Fashion designer Hubert de Givenchy and other stylish French homeowners seem to prefer pleated silk shades with short-fringed trim along their bottoms. Other suitable trims, though, include those with dangling little glass orbs or tiny wooden beads.

While most of the major fabric houses have trim departments, there are also companies whose sole business is passementerie. Samuel & Sons Passementerie, an American purveyor of trimmings and embellishments, designs a wide range of passementerie that has a slightly relaxed, American aesthetic to it, while Paris-based Houlès carries high-style, high-fashion passementerie that wouldn't look out of place on a couture gown.

 PATCHWORK

WHAT PATTERN SEEMS MORE TRUE-BLUE AMERICAN, NOT TO mention fitting for a Ralph Lauren ad, than patchwork? Think of those patchwork calico dresses worn by pioneer women or even that most prominent example of Americana, the patchwork quilt. But patchwork doesn't have to be so country casual. When rendered in sophisticated fabrics and contemporary colors, patchwork seems better suited for today's dwellings than yesteryear's homes on the range.

During the 1960s, patchwork joined the ranks of the fashion-forward thanks to Yves Saint Laurent and his elegant yet bohemian evening gowns made of patch-worked silk fabrics. On New York's Seventh Avenue, American designer Adolfo had a runway hit on his hands with patchwork skirts that became all the rage among the ladies-who-lunch set.

A modern version of the patchwork rug can offer presence and pattern to an unassuming floor, but because of its monochromatic patches, it won't overwhelm surrounding furnishings.

In fact, some of Adolfo's skirts were sewn from real patchwork quilts belonging to designer Gloria Vanderbilt, a woman whose passion for quilts and patchwork literally

knew no bounds. In a now famous Horst P. Horst photograph, Vanderbilt was snapped in sartorial splendor, a vibrant patchwork gown replete with an Elizabethan-style ruffled collar, while seated on the floor of her bedroom, a room whose floors were decorated with varnished patches of contrasting fabrics and whose walls, ceiling, and doors were covered in a phalanx of patchwork quilts. And the finishing touch? Why, a bed dressed with both a patchwork quilted spread and bed skirt, of course.

There's no denying that Vanderbilt's bedroom was memorable, but for most of us, such patchwork exuberance might prove to be overwhelming. Far more agreeable, and even more modern looking too, are printed fabrics that hint at rather than imitate the look of patchwork, doing so in subtle tonal ways. Clarence House's African Patchwork linen fabric is a medley of different tribal patterns rendered in earthy tones, while Brunschwig & Fils carries a patchwork print called Devon Woven Patchwork that looks like a map of blue-and-cream-patterned territories outlined in wavy borders. Not only are these fabrics attractive, they also add full-bodied interest and visual depth to whatever they adorn. Think of it as instant layering, achieved through the use of just a single fabric.

Patchwork rugs are classic floor coverings, but rather than those that invoke the American pioneer spirit, try one that summons up sophistication. Currently popular are those rugs woven of calf-hair squares, usually available in a rainbow of colors, such as the impressive array carried by Kyle Bunting Rugs. Remember, though, that the more color contrast there is between neighboring patches, the more robust the patchwork effect. If you prefer something with more uniformity, then choose rugs composed of patches rendered in strongly similar, or perhaps even the same, colors.

P | PLASTER FURNISHINGS

FEW DECORATIVE MATERIALS BETTER CAPTURE THE STYLIZED glamour of the 1930s than plaster, especially when used to dramatic effect. With its chalky-white finish that, when light shines upon it, amplifies its surface decoration, plaster was like putty in the hands of that era's designers as they molded it into lamps, tables, and wall adornments. When placed alongside the decade's other stylish favorites, sparkling mirror and slippery-looking satin, plaster furnishings helped to infuse interiors with a sense of theatricality, a contrasting scene of light and shadow as well as dullness and polish.

Two of the most prominent plaster artists of the 1930s were the Giacometti brothers, Alberto and Diego, whose plaster lamps and vases were championed by the sophisticated set, most notably famed French designer Jean-Michel Frank. Then there were the famous Serge Roche–designed plaster torchères in the shape of palm trees as well as palm-frond-looking plaster mirrors conceived by designer Emilio Terry, both of which counted designers Frances Elkins and Syrie Maugham as fans. And although plaster may have hit its decorative peak in the 1930s, it found renewed popularity in the 1960s and 1970s thanks to California designer John Dickinson's tables and chairs, which were supported by chunky plaster paw-footed legs.

SEE ALSO
*Hoofs,
Claws, and
Paws; Satin;
Torchères.*

What made plaster so alluring in the 1930s is still more or less the same today. Plaster's pure-white coloration not only allows it to live among a variety of colors and prints but also provides your eyes with a place to rest. If you choose to paper a room's walls in a busy print, add a plaster table or wall sconce as a moment of relief from the surrounding pattern, something that will elicit a relaxing "Ahhh" from your eyes.

Plaster lamps can be rather expressive-looking accessories, striking a note of drama on the tables upon which they rest. When lit, it's all surface peaks and moody shadows, enlivening what is otherwise a plain visage. And we mustn't overlook plaster's matte finish, a pleasant departure from the polished wood and lacquered painted finishes that can be found in many homes. It's this juxtaposition between plaster and contrasting finishes and colors that sparks interest in a room. Remember, though, that only a piece or two of plaster is needed for dramatic flair. Anything more and it will lose its impact.

PLASTER IN FASHION

In the 1930s and '40s, some very tony shops and salons got plastered in over-the-top decorations, which were intended to create fantasy settings so customers could indulge in luxurious retail therapy.

Jean-Michel Frank and his band of merry artisans decorated some of Paris's most fabulous couture salons, including that of Lucien Lelong, whose perfume room had plaster-dipped draperies hanging between doors and perfume displays. Equally as splendid was the Frank-designed showroom of Elsa Schiaparelli, which was appointed with cornucopia-shaped vases, a giant bowl-shaped ceiling light, and a shell-shaped floor lamp, all of which were rendered in plaster by Alberto Giacometti.

Helena Rubinstein outfitted her Fifth Avenue, New York, skincare salon in dramatic fashion, most notably with a bullion-fringed borne (a round sofa with an upholstered pillar in the middle) that was topped by a massive plaster urn. But the most theatrical of all had to be the Coty Salon in Manhattan, where Dorothy Draper created a tented perfume bar with a plaster, plumed central pole and a big top of draped white satin.

P | PORTIERES

YOU MIGHT NOT BE FAMILIAR WITH THE WORD *PORTIERE,* BUT IF you've watched your fair share of old movies, you've probably seen one or two and not even realized it. Remember those scenes in which two people were seated in, say, a drawing room or conservatory where they were discussing a top-secret plan or engaging in amorous activity, while unbeknownst to them, they were being spied upon by someone hiding behind a curtain that was framing a doorway? Well, that curtain was a portiere providing surreptitious cover for the spy, gossip, or third person in a love triangle character.

Portieres have long played dual roles in decorating, serving both a practical and a prettifying purpose. In homes with great halls and grand entryways, living spaces were often accessed through wide thresholds that lacked doors. (In fact, the same often holds true for houses built on much smaller scales.) To compensate for the absence of doors, curtains were hung at the outer edges of the opening to help ward off cold drafts as well as to visually soften the transition between rooms. And appropriately enough, these door curtains were named *portieres,* the feminine form of the French word for porter.

Although perhaps not as common today, portieres remain an attractive solution to the often vexing problem of what to do with doorless

A Tony Duquette print fabric, "Tibetan Sun" from Jim Thompson, makes a striking portiere that softens the transition between rooms. When pulled to cover the opening, it protects the living room beyond from drafts.

doorways. My bedroom has a walk-through closet leading to the bathroom, and every night when I get into bed, staring me in the face are rows of shoes and coat hangers. A more pleasing view could certainly be achieved if I were to hang pretty curtain panels at the closet opening, which would help to partially hide the inner workings of my wardrobe.

Perhaps you have an entry hall that serves as a precursor to the rest of your home. Why not add a portiere or two, done up in a snazzy fabric, of course, between the hall and what lies beyond to build a chic sense of anticipation? Alternatively, let's say your living room or dining room walls are pockmarked with multiple doors. You could remove one of the superfluous doors and replace it with a pair of portieres made of the same fabric as your window curtains, which would help to open up your room and make it feel less closed off from the rest of the house.

The Victorian era had an unfortunate love affair with portieres, one that often resulted in overwrought, contorted velvet curtains. Steer clear of such oppressiveness, and stick to simple portieres, perhaps embellished with some type of tailored trim, that either hang straight to the ground or can be softly gathered with tiebacks. One portiere will suffice for a small space (hang it from a curtain rod and rings so that you can draw it when you want to completely cover the opening), while a pair is preferable for large areas. Who knows? You might like the effect so much that you institute an open-door policy throughout your entire house.

SEE ALSO
Passementerie.

P | POTPOURRI

THE 1980S WERE NOT KIND TO POTPOURRI, POLLUTING ITS DRIED flowers and herbs with overbearing scents that, although popular back then, seem something to sneeze at today. But don't let bad memories cloud your judgment. Thanks to today's more natural, earthy-scented potpourri, this fragrant concoction remains an easy, not to mention attractive, way to keep your house smelling its best.

If you enjoy the aroma of potpourri but don't care for its dried appearance, consider using a potpourri urn, which works as a decorative diffuser that hides the fragrant floral concoction from both sight and dust.

Agraria's Bitter Orange potpourri has been the gold standard of potpourri for decades now. With its sophisticated spicy aroma, it's no wonder that Bitter Orange has earned the moniker "Park Avenue Potpourri." Also popular is potpourri from the venerable Italian brand Santa Maria Novella; theirs is a blend of hand-picked flowers and herbs from the Florentine countryside. Santa Maria Novella also makes deodorant for cats and dogs (rose for the felines and white musk for the canines), so if your pet is the culprit of your home's unpleasant smell, then you might want to consider investing in some of that too.

SEE ALSO
Flowers;
Scented
Candles.

While an attractive silver bowl or ceramic compote of potpourri adds a homey touch to a room, it unfortunately tends to collect dust like crazy. One option is to change your potpourri on a regular basis, but even better is to place it in an antique or vintage potpourri urn. These lidded containers, often made of porcelain, earthenware, or even metal, have pierced holes that allow the potpourri's fragrance to dissipate while protecting it from dust. Some potpourri urns are ornate, while others aren't quite so grand. Mottahedeh, the noted china manufacturer, has made some charming potpourri containers over the years that are worth searching for online and at tag sales.

Then again, you can always forgo the expense of store-bought potpourri, as well as flowers and candles, for that matter, and scent your home in more frugal ways. Philanthropist Bunny Mellon was known to have her household staff boil apples on the stove to create a pleasant aroma, while the late magazine editor and writer Fleur Cowles took a similar approach by boiling cloves in water and then meandering through her house with the pot to spread the spicy fragrance. You can even perfume your house with the same scent that you use on your body. If you've ever wondered what to do with that unused bath oil sitting next to your tub, take a cue from the late Estée Lauder. She reportedly dabbed her lamps' light bulbs with cotton balls soaked in her signature Youth Dew bath oil, the lamps' warmth helping to distribute the oil's scent throughout her home.

P | POUFS

WHILE THE WORD *POUF* MAY CONJURE UP CRINGE-WORTHY MEMO-ries of those bubble-skirted dresses that were all the rage a few decades ago, don't let the name mislead you when it comes to décor. Furni-ture poufs, which are low to the ground and lack a back and arms, are not just timeless but handy, too, proving their mettle at parties, where additional seating is often a requirement.

Similar to ottomans, although, well, pouffier thanks to their often cushiony upholstered tops, poufs are a relaxed accompaniment to today's more casual style of living and entertaining. One of the more popular versions in recent years has been the Moroccan pouf, a squat, round leather-covered cushion that usually features embroidered designs. Despite the fact that they remind me of those old-timey leather medicine balls, Moroccan poufs are useful and firm enough to support a range of body sizes, and yet, because of their rather diminu-tive height, they can be stored under cocktail or side tables when not in use.

My favorite example is what is sometimes referred to as a "Turk-ish ottoman" although it is very much a

One of the more exotic-looking poufs, the Turkish ottoman consists of two upholstered cushions that behave as a sturdy tuffet for sitting or foot propping.

167

SEE ALSO
Exotic Prints.

pouf. Resembling two square cushions placed crosswise one on top of the other, Turkish ottomans are most associated with designers Billy Baldwin and Angelo Donghia, both of whom used these poufs in the most glamorous of settings. The beauty of this particular pouf, and really other versions as well, is that its personality changes depending on its upholstery. Cover your pouf in an exotic-looking print, say, a pink ikat like that which Billy Baldwin once chose for a fashion designer client, and it will be fit for a Persian queen like Scheherazade. But choose a proper stripe or a snappy geometric print, and your pouf will look made for Park Avenue.

And although it might seem pure folly, a pouf, specifically a low-rider version with the shortest of feet, makes an excellent, not to mention indulgent, dog bed, the perfect perch from which your pet can rule the roost.

GLOBAL STYLE

Whether it's a home in Morocco, a Turkish-style room, or a wardrobe of caftans, exoticism has long found favor among the sophisticated set, especially those with artistic talents and, more often than not, means.

One of the most ardent devotees of exoticism was early-twentieth-century French couturier Paul Poiret. Not only did he revolutionize women's fashion by dressing them in harem pants (remember the uproar that Lady Sybil caused on *Downton Abbey* when she wore a pair?), he even threw a well-publicized costume party, "The Thousand and Second Night." In fact, the fashion world seems to have a longstanding love affair with the exotic, most notably Yves Saint Laurent and Pierre Bergé, whose house and garden in Marrakech, Morocco, remains one of the most talked-about domestic oases in design history.

Then there was heiress Doris Duke, whose real-life Hawaiian Shangri-La was named just that, *Shangri La*. Built in the 1930s, the estate has a pronounced Middle Eastern flavor, with furnishings and architecture influenced by Syrian, Moroccan, and Iranian culture. And very apropos: Duke chose velvet-covered poufs to accompany her low-to-the-ground dining table.

P PRINT ROOMS

ONE OF THE MORE UNIQUE DECORATIVE TRENDS TO HAVE EMERGED
in the late eighteenth century was that of the print room, a style made
fashionable by young English gentlemen returning home from their
"Grand Tours of Europe." Souvenirs from these journeys often
included caches of black-and-white engravings, or prints, that depicted
any number of subjects, including architecture and gardens. When
faced with the challenge of how best to display these engravings back
home, some clever person fell upon the idea of pasting the unframed
prints directly onto the walls of a room and embellishing them with
monochromatic paper borders, garlands, ropes, and swags, all of which
gave the effect of decoratively hung prints. And so the print room came
into vogue, dedicated to this decorative display of engravings.

Although the Grand Tour is not easily feasible today, print rooms
continue to enchant those seeking traditional flair in their homes. The
late Charles de Beistegui, mentioned yet again due to his temerity in
decorating, installed a print breakfast room at his Château de Groussay.
And British designer John Stefanidis, in collaboration with his clients,
once devised a print room turret, one outfitted and used for serving
drinks to guests. But while this decorative wall treatment is steeped in
British tradition, it's equally delightful on American shores too.

SEE ALSO
Stencils.

What makes the concept of the print room so appealing is that the room is so tidy looking. Traditionally, the walls of a print room were painted in shades of straw or pale yellow, blue, or green, all subtle colors that balanced out the graphically toned engravings. And, more important, the thematically cohesive prints and their paper embellishments were always adhered to the wall in a symmetrical, orderly fashion. If you find the current craze for walls littered with random assemblages of artwork to be dubious, then a print room just might be for you.

If you're highly ambitious, you could create your print room in the old-fashioned, authentic way. However, that's not a requirement anymore thanks to wallpaper firms that produce print room paper. ARC Collections Ltd., a London-based manufacturer, produces a wonderful range of papers, and fabrics too, that mimic the look of a classic print room, one boasting prints of garden urns and statuary. Also based in England is Lewis & Wood, whose droll version of print room wallpaper features French engravings that, according to the firm's website, follow "the path of courtly seduction." Or you could take the partly homemade approach by pasting your collection of engravings directly to the wall, enriching each print with decorative borders, frames, and garlands painted with the aid of a stencil.

No matter how you achieve your print room, just remember that the room's other furnishings should be simple so as not to compete with its embellished walls. In print rooms, it's the walls that bear the decorative load rather than what lies within them.

In a traditional print room, frameless engravings are affixed directly to the wall, as are paper embellishments that imply frames, ropes and rings, and other picture-hanging hardware.

QUOTATIONS AND WITTICISMS

QUOTATIONS AND QUIPS ARE SPLASHED EVERYWHERE THESE DAYS, from social networking sites to the t-shirt on one's back. But in few places does their presence impart as much flair as in the home, where a favorite quotation, decoratively displayed, will serve to amuse and perhaps even elicit a chuckle or two.

Pillows seem prime targets for wordy flourishes. At her home in France, Elsie de Wolfe filled an entire banquette with silk throw pillows that had been embroidered with such quips as "It takes a stout heart to live without roots," as well as the now famous "Never complain, never explain." And the acid-tongued Alice Roosevelt Longworth, daughter of Theodore Roosevelt, had a pillow stitched with her now infamous saying "If you can't say something good about someone, sit right here by me." If you ask me, that pillow spelled a dangerous proposition.

When embroidered on a pillow, a droll quotation by Diana Vreeland, seen here, can inject a controlled dose of wit and humor into a room without seeming silly.

The Duchess of Windsor also let her accessories do the talking. Her collection of mementos included a framed, painted quotation that read, "Girl old enough to know better would like to meet man not quite that old." Wallis was certainly ahead of her time, as

Unshined shoes are the end of civilization

this quote seems positively made for one's profile page on an online dating website.

Silver picture frames, bowls, loving cups, and trays are all auspicious accessories for engraved sentiments, especially those that express nostalgia or tender feelings. Silver barware, on the other hand, can benefit from the leavening effects of quotations that are fizzy, sparkling, and even downright naughty. Writer Dorothy Parker's oft-quoted "One more drink and I'll be under the host" is destined to appear on a cocktail shaker, if it hasn't done so already.

The knack to sprinkling your home with quotations is to show restraint. As Noel Coward retorted, "Wit ought to be a glorious treat like caviar; never spread it about like marmalade." Limit wordy gestures to one type of accessory, and then corral your quota together into one space, much as de Wolfe did with her pillows. And remember, while a few quotations are witty, anything more unfortunately looks comical.

 SAID WHO?

Many legendary tastemakers had wits that matched their outsize personalities and their self-assured style. Bon mots and quips simply rolled off their tongues and attained quotable status soon after. Did their flip comments really just come to them at the spur of the moment? Or were these comments just one component of their carefully cultivated façades? I suppose that we'll never know.

"People who eat white bread have no dreams." —*Diana Vreeland*

"To be in fashion is to be already passé." —*Jean Cocteau*

"It takes a lot of work to look relaxed." —*Nan Kempner*

"As long as you know that most men are like children you know everything." —*Coco Chanel*

"Women dress alike all over the world: they dress to be annoying to other women." —*Elsa Schiaparelli*

R | ROCK CRYSTAL

WITH A PIOUS HISTORY THAT INCLUDES APPEARANCES IN centuries-old Christian reliquaries, rock crystal, a colorless form of the mineral quartz, continues to play a role in decoration, one that while not quite as saintly is no less virtuous. With its intriguing and almost transparent appearance, rock crystal adds an element of natural wonderment to one's home, a rara avis among your more run-of-the-mill accessories.

Lamps and chandeliers are the most common accents in which to find rock crystal, appropriate considering that you can best appreciate this mineral's ice-like appearance when it is cast in light. Chandeliers, both antique and new, often have drops of rock crystal that hang like baubles, further ornamenting an already ornamental fixture. You can find both rock crystal table lamps and candlesticks that look like glimmering chunks of frozen water, all fire and ice, as well as wall sconces bearing carved rock crystal flowers, for example, or tropical birds.

For those who consider most trifles to be trifling, rock crystal objects often meet with a seal of approval, regarded as sophisticated table accents that lack tchotchke overtones. Coco Chanel, known for her restrained sense of style, was a noted collector of rock crystal bibelots as was Brooke Astor, who owned one of the most delightful rock

You can really appreciate the ice-like appearance of this rock crystal lamp because of its placement against an eggplant-colored wall. Rock crystal has a luxurious nature that begs to be mixed with sumptuous, glamorous accessories.

SEE ALSO
Sconces.

crystal objects that I have seen: a carved rock crystal dachshund, attired with gold collar and ruby eyes and placed upon an opalescent quartz and gold tasseled cushion. While many vintage examples of these objects can be prohibitively expensive, especially considering that they were often designed with precious mounts and gemstones, rock crystal doesn't have to be limited to those with big budgets. More affordable are those organic-shaped pieces of clear quartz that are less decorative and more like mineral specimens, not to mention those small, obelisk-shaped examples that look like they could be talismans of some mystical tribe. And because rock crystal is rumored to ward off negative energy, the more you collect of rock crystal, the more positive effect it might have on your home.

ROCK STAR

Rock crystal's mesmerizing personality seems made for sublime decorations, and few rock crystal pieces are more dazzling than those highly sought-after Mystery Clocks by Cartier.

Developed by the famed jeweler in the early twentieth century, the Mystery Clock features rock crystal disks upon which the clock's hands are mounted, giving the appearance of hands floating on the clock's face. The clock's inner gears and mechanisms are hidden within other parts of the clock, which only adds to the mystery of how this clock really works. Needless to say, such elaborate construction has meant that the cost to produce such pieces is expensive.

Over the years, there have been a limited number of Mystery Clocks produced by Cartier, with each version more dazzling than the last. There is the Mystery Clock that depicts a Moghul pavilion and elephant, which is comprised of rose quartz, agate, gemstones, and, of course, rock crystal. Equally as exotic-looking is the clock that is reminiscent of an Egyptian temple portico, one with rock crystal columns and a gold, diamond, and black enamel–spotted panther.

And one of the most spectacular examples of this clock has to be that with white gold and pavé-diamond polar bears resting upon rock crystal icebergs and blue hardstone water.

RUSH MATTING AND SISAL

"WHEN PRETTY IS TOO PRETTY, YOUR AUDIENCE IS GOING TO BE conscious of flutter and lace and everything trailing." Although she was referring to fashion, designer Claire McCardell's wisdom could be applied to interior design as well. Too much prettiness, grandness, or perfection can spoil the intended effect, robbing a house of warmth and charm. If delusions of grandeur are threatening your house, it's time to foil the pomp with something rough and tumble: rush matting and sisal.

British design legend John Fowler often chose rush matting, a floor covering woven of dried rushes, for the cavernous English country houses that he decorated. He used these natural, casual rugs to counteract the majestic and at times intimidating architecture that distinguishes many of these houses. In fact, decades later rush matting is still a common floor embellishment in both grand and quaint country houses alike, its humble demeanor adding an easygoing warmth to the sometimes chilly English countryside.

In this country, it is sisal, also made of woven natural fibers, rather than rush matting that is most often found in homes, a well-suited, not to mention well-priced, floor covering for our relaxed American sensibility. (Rush matting can cost a pretty penny.) Not only is sisal effective

in toning down any inkling of formality in a room, it also helps to bridge the gap between traditional and contemporary furnishings, both of which look striking, and quite compatible, when placed upon sisal. You could equate this natural carpet to a pair of tailored blue jeans: both are now considered to be appropriate for casual and dressy establishments alike.

If you have floors that are in less than great shape and you can't afford to refinish them, consider having sisal installed wall to wall as an economical solution. Whereas neutral-toned sisal is unobtrusive and thus versatile, dyed sisal, now available in a host of vibrant colors, is an alternative for those who want their floors to look prominent. And to help soften sisal's natural coarseness, try placing an area rug or two upon it. The mingling of floor coverings not only will provide tactile pleasure but will add textural interest to your floors as well.

As versatile as sisal and rush matting can be, they are best avoided in homes with young children and pets. Babies crawling around on this rough woven material are liable to get bad cases of rug burn, while a dog's accident can ruin sisal in the blink of an eye. In fact, most liquids are generally harmful to sisal, but not so with rush matting. The occasional sprinkling of water over rush matting will keep it both fresh and flexible, ensuring its use for decades to come.

A natural-colored sisal rug, which works effortlessly with both casual and formal furnishings, creates harmony between an elegant drinks table and a comfortable upholstered chair.

SATIN

"THE WORD THAT ALMOST MAKES ME THROW UP IS SATIN. DAMASK
makes me throw up." So said Billy Baldwin, a designer who perhaps let
his passion for cotton prejudice him against silky satin. But we need
look no further than a woman's closet to see that among the cotton,
linen, and wool, it's satin that dazzles our eyes, a glamorous attention
getter among mundane fabrics.

Watch any of the movie musicals or fizzy, high-style comedies from
the 1930s or 1940s, and you'll probably see the film's characters wearing satin, sleeping on satin, or drinking cocktails and rattling off witty
dialogue while seated on satin-covered chairs. The shimmery fabric
wasn't restricted to movie sets either. Even in the average home, satin
upholstery was considered to be perfectly acceptable in its more public
rooms, while behind closed doors, quilted satin bedspreads were found
in many master bedrooms.

Although less commonly found in today's living and dining rooms,
satin continues to be favored for bedrooms, where a judicious use of it
can impart both glossy glamour and femininity to the space. (Despite
his aversion to satin, Billy Baldwin did say that both women *and* men
like a feminine bedroom.) Quilted satin coverlets in soft, subtle colors
look smashing when folded neatly at the end of the bed. Or what about a

*Once a staple in
stylish bedrooms
of the 1930s
(not to mention
movie sets), a
satin quilt—so
quintessentially
feminine—is still
a glamorous bed
covering after all
of these years.*

SATIN CONTINUES TO BE FAVORED FOR BEDROOMS, WHERE A JUDICIOUS USE OF IT CAN IMPART BOTH GLOSSY GLAMOUR AND FEMININITY TO THE SPACE.

quilted satin throw to use when napping on a chaise longue or daybed? Elsie de Wolfe was known to order *couvre-pieds* for her female clients. These nifty little throws, sewn of quilted silk on one side and white fur on the other, were made to cover a lady's feet while she was stretched out reading or having her hair coiffed.

Another luxurious use of satin is on quilted bed jackets, an affordable luxury that keeps you quite warm and toasty when reading in bed on a chilly night. Visit Leontine Linens' website, and you'll find exquisite satin bed jackets and quilts, too, which are very tempting. And while we're on the subject of beds, have you seen those handy quilted satin bed caddies, designed by Ann Gish, that are meant to hang from between your mattress and box spring? The pocketed end can hold remote controls, glasses, and anything else you might need while lounging in bed.

If you're going to the expense of assembling a well-appointed wardrobe, why not take care of it in a well-appointed closet? Satin-padded clothes hangers, available in a rainbow of colors, are gentle on your clothes, while satin shoe bags protect your off-season footwear from dust. And why not invest in some monogrammed satin lingerie bags, also available through Leontine Linens, that will prevent your delicates from being snagged by wooden drawers?

When it comes to satin upholstery, though, whether in the bedroom or another room, moderation is key. Small bedroom furniture like boudoir chairs or vanity stools looks smashing when covered in a sturdier satin like duchesse. Leave the large items like sofas, curtains, and headboards to a fabric that is a little less shiny.

SEE ALSO
Quilted Fabrics.

SCENIC WALLPAPER

OF ALL THE DECORATIONS THAT HAVE STORIES TO TELL, FEW do so with as much narrative as scenic wallpaper. Conceived in late eighteenth-century Europe as an alternative to painted murals, scenic wallpaper is typically composed of a series of hand-printed or, at times, hand-painted panels, each one depicting a unique scene. When placed together in their intended succession on the walls of a room, these non-repetitive panels create a panoramic effect, making one feel as though standing in a seamless foreign vista or witnessing a historic event.

What gives scenic wallpaper such novelty and charm is that it often portrays notable moments in history—and in exuberant fashion too. Battle scenes, exploration of the New World, Napoléon's funeral, and architectural monuments have all been immortalized on such wall-paper, but that's not to say that bucolic landscapes aren't popular too. In fact, one of the more popular scenic wallpapers is Le Palais-Royale, an animated scene of garden follies set against a bright-blue backdrop and a colonnaded foreground. It was this wallpaper that designer Frances Elkins ultimately chose to grace the walls of Casa Amesti, her home in Montecito, California.

Thankfully, there are manufacturers that continue to design and print such paper today, including de Gournay, Gracie, Fromental, and,

SEE ALSO
Screens.

the granddaddy of them all, Zuber & Cie, the French factory that has been producing wallpaper since 1797. Jacqueline Kennedy was so taken with one particular Zuber scenic paper, Views of North America, that she had the White House Diplomatic Reception Room papered in it, where it remains intact today.

Speaking of public rooms, it was Elsie de Wolfe who once advised that scenic paper be limited to those rooms like the hallway where "one doesn't loiter." Dining rooms, now used somewhat infrequently, are also popular venues for such paper. However, I find this paper so beguiling that I could live with it in my living room or bedroom without becoming overwhelmed by its scenery. Another consideration, especially given the costliness of this paper, is whether you want to paper all four walls of a room or simply one, a penny-wise decision that won't look pound fool-ish. Because of the versatility of this paper, you can order an abridged version of a panorama, say, two or three successive scenes, rather the entire vista, and the effect won't be any less striking or comprehensible.

Then again, if you are currently living in a dwelling that isn't your "forever home," consider buying a few panels, perhaps antique exam-ples found at auction or newly printed ones, and either frame them individually as art or mount them onto wooden folding screens, both of which you can take with you should you move.

A single antique wallpaper panel, which depicts a man fishing along the shore as the ship, Ste. Marie, sails by, was affixed to a wooden board so that it could be decoratively hung from a wall.

SCENTED CANDLES

THE DESIRE FOR A PLEASANT-SMELLING ENVIRONMENT HAS BEEN on the minds of homeowners for centuries. Did you know that at the palace of Louis XV, doves whose wings had been saturated in perfume were allowed to fly throughout the halls, their flapping wings helping to disperse the scent? It isn't any surprise that the court of Louis XV was referred to as the "Perfumed Court."

Fortunately for us, we've come a long way since the days of using our feathered friends as fragrance diffusers. Although we now have all kinds of means for scenting our homes, it's the scented candle that ranks as one of the most popular. Visit any chic dwelling, and you'll probably find a scented candle burning on an entrance hall table, where its scent makes a good first impression upon guests. Living rooms, libraries, and powder rooms are also choice venues for candles, as are bedrooms. (However, if you're planning to burn candles in your bedroom for, um, amorous purposes, please don't light a battalion of them. One wrong move and your curtains might go up in flames.)

Thanks to the staggering num-

One of the more ubiquitous (and most popular) decorative accessories in chic homes, the scented candle is practically a requirement for gracious living and one that infuses a home with its alluring, inviting fragrance.

ber of candle brands available today, candle shopping can prove overwhelming. Keep sniffing and you're sure to find one that suits your taste. Some of my favorites are D. Porthault's Summer candle (a floral scent that is the essence of femininity), Japanese Quince by Seda France (its toile-patterned container makes it perfect for gift giving), and Votivo's Mandarin (a clean citrus scent that, when burned in the kitchen, helps to eliminate cooking odors).

No discussion of candles would be complete without mentioning Rigaud, one of the earliest purveyors of scented candles. Back in the go-go 1980s, style mavens everywhere placed Rigaud's signature glass votives with their metal lids conspicuously in their Park Avenue apartments or their suburban manses. Out of all of Rigaud's various fragrances, it was Cyprès, the green-colored candle with the pine scent, that was most coveted. Rigaud fans are legion, and their names read like the Social Register and International Best-Dressed List all wrapped into one: Jacqueline Kennedy; Grace Kelly; Gloria Vanderbilt; and Diana Vreeland, whose husband, Reed, was the American representative for Rigaud. The bonus that comes with buying a Rigaud candle is the fabulous black-and-white-striped box in which it is packaged. Do as Diana Vreeland, who treated these boxes as smart-looking pencil holders for her desk while editor at *Vogue*.

S SCONCES

ALTHOUGH THE WALL-HANGING CANDLE SCONCE MIGHT BE A sentimental favorite for its old-fashioned, romantic glow, it is the electrified version, usually hardwired to the wall, that is the more practical solution for lighting a room, especially when partnered with table lamps and ceiling fixtures. When used in pairs, flanking a powder room mirror, a painting over a fireplace, or a sofa, for example, sconces provide soft yet robust washes of light, strong enough by which to see and still diffuse enough to be flattering. And in small halls, entryways, or recesses in which table lamps are not an option and chandeliers might seem overkill, a pair of wall sconces will help to cast light on what might otherwise be a dark situation.

As practical as wall sconces may be, their appearances can, at times, be quite fanciful, running the gamut from sparkling crystal to opulent ormolu. You can find sconces in the shapes of lyres, stars, birds, feathers, and leaves, not to mention in designs that are best described as swooshes and swirls. For those with a Spartan sensibility, there are many

Looking like they are reaching out from the wall with bulbs in hand, a pair of wall sconces illuminate the wall from which they hang while also jazzing it up with decorative flair.

examples of sconces that are little more than plain brass or chrome wall plates holding sturdy little arms, most striking in their simplicity. And speaking of arms, one of my favorite sconces has an arm that extends from the wall plate to resemble a stylized human arm and hand in miniature. Because the hand is holding a lightbulb, when lit up it looks as if it's trying to pass the torch.

SEE ALSO
Candlelight.

Whether you're an avid reader or simply a couch potato, swing-arm lamp sconces attached to the wall just above each end of a sofa are immensely useful, especially considering that their hinged arms allow them to be positioned where light is needed, perhaps over your shoulder as you read. The classic swing-arm lamp, conceived by George Hansen in the 1940s, was so simple in its design, little more than a square metal wall plate to which a metal arm was hinged, and yet it has remained the gold standard of this lamp style to this day, proof that the best design is oftentimes the least affected.

Don't forget that many sconces require shades, which not only helps to control light but also adds decorative flair. Half shades, which basically look like shades sliced vertically in half, are made for those sconces in which the arms project only slightly from the wall, while small, full shades are appropriate for the rest. Ornate sconces can accommodate elaborate shades like those trimmed in tiny beads or fringe, while more austere sconces look best when topped with a neutral-colored paper or linen shade. And those swing-arm lamps that are always in good taste? It doesn't get any better than an Empire-style shade made of white lacquered paper, a favorite shade choice of both Billy Baldwin and Albert Hadley.

SCREENS

OF ALL FURNITURE, IT'S THE EXPANSIVE FLOOR SCREEN THAT HAS the greatest capacity to hide a multitude of sins. Often composed of multiple hinged panels, the screen can alternately serve as a cunning concealment, a picturesque partition, or simply a delightful decoration, . . . and sometimes, it's been to known to perform all three roles at once.

A screen's simple construction allows it to be dressed in any number of decorative finishes: upholstered in fabric or leather, wallpapered, decoratively painted, or even sheathed in mirror. One mirrored screen in particular, which Syrie Maugham designed in the 1930s, became an instant legend, its daring façade of vertiginously narrow strips of mirror a reflection of that era's thirst for glamour. Equally as coveted by connoisseurs is the Coromandel screen, an Oriental masterpiece typically decorated with a dark lacquered background and gold-painted scenes. Coco Chanel was so captivated by Coromandel screens that she eventually owned more than twenty of them!

The beauty of screens lies not just in their looks but in their ability to cover up anything that you don't want your guests to see. Dining rooms used to be a natural habitat for screens, typically placed by the kitchen door, where they hid the frenzy of food prep. For a more

To cozy up my living room, I placed two three-paneled upholstered screens behind my sofa. The screens' fabric, "Duquetterie" by Hutton Wilkinson for Jim Thompson, pays homage to its namesake, legendary designer Tony Duquette.

THE SCREEN CAN ALTERNATELY SERVE AS A CUNNING CONCEALMENT, A PICTURESQUE PARTITION, OR SIMPLY A DELIGHTFUL DECORATION.

modern use, place an attractive screen in front of any small, doorless room or corner in your house that may serve as a messy catchall for odds and ends to shield the disarray from the prying eyes of guests.

Exposed pipes and radiators can be the bane of old homes, where they have a tendency to stick out like sore thumbs. It's screens to the rescue in these situations too. Place a tall screen in a room's corner to hide floor-to-ceiling pipes, while a short, three-paneled screen can be situated in front of radiators and even under wall-mounted sinks to mask their visible pipes. These low screens can also fill dark voids in fireplaces when they're not in use.

Architecturally speaking, screens can be employed to create walls where there are none. If your home has one large space that serves as a living and dining room, you might want to create the illusion of two separate rooms by placing a pair of screens in the middle as a kind of wall, with a space in between the screens to serve as a pseudo-doorway. The same concept can be applied to studio apartments, where a screen can help to maintain privacy in one's sleeping area, for example.

Considering that Chanel had such a penchant for screens, it's worth taking a design cue from her and situating a screen behind a lengthy sofa, just as she did in her Paris salon. Not only does the screen's place-ment eliminate the need to buy art for the sofa wall, but it acts as a lavish backdrop for living too.

SINGERIES

DURING THE MIDDLE AGES, THE MONKEY OCCASIONALLY MADE decorative appearances in paintings and illuminated manuscripts, usually depicted as a sinister little creature. Come the seventeenth century, though, and monkeys began to play fashionable and less frightening roles in Western decorative arts, starring in their very own style, known as *singerie,* the French term for monkey decoration. Typically seen on the walls of decoratively painted rooms but also found on tapestries and furniture, *singeries* featured monkeys aping humans, dressed in fancy costumes and performing human tasks. It was not uncommon to see elaborate murals showing frocked monkeys as merrymakers, musicians, sculptors and painters, soldiers, and even hairdressers. The most noted examples of *singeries* are those created in the eighteenth century by French artist Christophe Huet for Château de Chantilly, France, where he painted two monkey rooms: La Grande Singerie and La Petite Singerie. In both rooms, walls and ceilings are adorned in a rococo frenzy of monkeys up to mischief making, their exuberance still enchanting visitors today.

Although the fad for *singeries* faded by the nineteenth century, our primate relatives did not stray too far from the world of decoration. Monkey motifs could be found among the Jazz Age speakeasies, appro-

priate venues considering the kind of monkey business that went on in such establishments. Manhattan's Monkey Bar, which dates back to 1936, still boasts original murals and light fixtures featuring, no surprise, monkeys. So how can monkeys make the leap from the walls of châteaux and Art Deco bars to our own homes? Through wallpaper, that's how. A room, especially a relatively small one, papered in whimsical monkeys never ceases to delight, which is the whole point of *singeries*. You could choose Scalamandré's Venetian Carnival, in which monkeys are kicking up their heels alongside Harlequins, or Schumacher's succinctly named Singeries, whose energetic monkeys are painting, sword fighting, and walking tightropes. But for a look that is more high-style and less capricious, consider de Gournay's stunning, Art Deco–inspired Deco Monkeys. The paper features monkeys being monkeys, swinging from branches without human clothing. Paper an entry hall, powder room, or alcove in Deco Monkeys for a whiff of simian chic.

While combing through bins at a charity flea market, I found this single roll of Schumacher's "Singeries" wallpaper, which proved just enough to paper a narrow sliver of a wall. The paper features frolicking monkeys walking on stilts and blowing bubbles.

 MONKEYING AROUND

Whereas dogs and cats conjure up warm and fuzzy feelings, monkeys imply impishness, a slightly naughty trait that guarantees the monkey's appearance on all kinds of lighthearted and frolicsome accessories, including:

BARWARE: Tiffany & Co.'s Sterling Silver Monkey Straw

STATIONERY: Gold Fancy Monkey Notecards from The Printery

DECORATIVE ACCESSORY: Mottahedeh white Monkey Bookends

FABRIC: Clarence House Jembala

DINNERWARE: Petit Singe White Monkey china by Juliska

SHOES: Stubbs & Wootton bespoke Darwin embroidered slippers

ART: Lalique clear crystal Monkey sculptures

SKIRTED TABLES

SKIRTED TABLES MAY NOT LOOK AS THOUGH THEY'RE OUTFITTED for hard work, but in reality, they are. Thanks to their ubiquitous cloths that are oh-so-practical, these tables are immensely useful, something that just might give new meaning to the term "dressed for success."

It's as secret hiding places that skirted tables are at their most handy. Have you ever scrambled around your house minutes before guests were to arrive, frantically searching for a place to hide those stacks of magazines, mail, or your pet's toys? If you have a skirted table at the ready, you can simply shove everything underneath its cloth. In fact, if you're pressed for storage space in your home, think of a skirted table as an attractive place under which to stow away off-season clothes (neatly in storage boxes, of course), computer equipment, and all of the other detritus of small-space living.

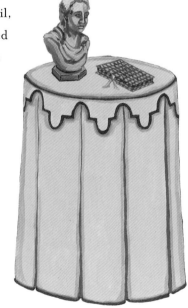

A skirted table, especially one that has a snappy scalloped topper, serves as a flattering cover-up for unattractive table legs as well as a hiding place for household odds and ends.

Perhaps you own a side table that has attractive qualities like proper height and size but is lacking in the looks department. Have a cloth made for the table, where it will serve to camouflage its deficiencies. While I search for my dream dining table, I have a round collapsible table that, when left undressed, looks rather unattractive. But concealed under a custom-made cloth, my ugly table becomes rather fetching—no longer a shameful-looking dining table that, at times, also serves as a repository for my latest design books.

Some people take issue with skirted tables due to those frilly, hoop-like skirts that were de rigueur decades ago. But a table skirt doesn't have to be flouncy, with some of the most appropriate, not to mention handsome, skirts being those that hang straight to the floor, lacking embellishment. A solid colored cotton or linen fabric is always a safe choice, while velvet and silk work best in more formal rooms. Prints should be used judiciously, as should trim. And skirts often look their most tailored, and sturdiest, when lined in cotton, although that's not always the case with silk. The beauty of a silk skirt is that it's light and delicate in appearance, as if one gust of wind will cause the table's skirt to fly up.

The table skirts that are the easiest to make might be like the ones seen so often in the libraries of English country houses. These skirts are little more than simple spreads of felt or wool that provide a protective surface upon which to place books, lamps, and other objects. Oftentimes these skirts don't even reach the floor but rather just skim the tops of table legs. A trip to your local fabric store will yield all kinds of solid-colored felts and woolens that can be used to create your own library table skirt, one that can be just cut to size rather than sewn.

SLIPCOVERS

FOR MUCH OF THE TWENTIETH CENTURY, IT WAS COMMON HOUSE-
hold practice to change the look of one's sofa and comfortable chairs
with seasonal slipcovers. Spring and summer usually entailed a solid or
gaily printed cotton fabric slipcover, while cooler months dictated cozy,
warm fabrics like woolens or velvets. In fact, Billy Baldwin followed this
domestic tradition, once boasting that the pale-blue denim fabric used
for his furniture's summer slipcovers cost him only 69 cents a yard!

Far from being extravagant, seasonal slipcovers make good sense.
Let's say you want to watch TV from your sofa on a sultry summer night.
What's more comfortable to lounge upon than crisp, cool cotton? That
same cotton loses some of its appeal, however, on a blustery night in
January, when all you want to do is snuggle up in toasty wool.

If your sofa is already upholstered in, say, a wintery fabric, you
might want to consider purchasing a cotton or linen slipcover for summertime use over the sofa's existing upholstery. Or you can have two
sets of seasonal slipcovers made, with the underlying sofa left in its
unfinished, un-upholstered state. The advantage to owning a pair of
slipcovers is that they can be laundered by a professional cleaner when
not in use. Custom-made slipcovers don't come cheap, but off-the-
shelf slipcovers are affordable.

*Once a household rite of spring, lightweight
furniture slipcovers—often made of gaily printed
cotton or linen—seasonally replaced heavier,
and sometimes masculine, winter versions.*

The other benefit of slipcovers is that they protect the furniture underneath them. If you have a pretty sofa upholstered in a delicate fabric, you might want to buy a premade cotton slipcover that can withstand the rigors of children and pets. Simply remove the slipcover before guests arrive. In many European country estates, you often see armchairs, especially those in libraries and sitting rooms, shrouded in well-worn cotton slipcovers. Not only do these slipcovers add a relaxed note to their elegant surroundings, they also protect the chair's underlying fabric from the wear and tear caused by long-term lounging and relaxing.

Finally, a slipcover is an effective disguise for furniture that is in less than great shape, buying you time before you have to visit the upholsterer. A rat-tatty upholstered chair can be given a facelift with a simple cotton slipcover purchased from Pottery Barn or Crate & Barrel. And many of the upholstered pieces available through Ballard Designs are made for slipcovers, so you can change the look of your sofa at whim—one day blue-and-cream check, the next, graphic black-and-white stripes.

But beware of those clear plastic slipcovers, famously used by actress Joan Crawford to maintain her furniture. Between those covers and her aversion to wire coat hangers, is it any wonder that she had a reputation for overzealous fastidiousness?

SLIPPER CHAIRS

ALTHOUGH NOW A FIXTURE IN MOST CONTEMPORARY FURNITURE lines, the slipper chair is actually a traditional form that dates back to eighteenth-century Europe, where, because of the chair's petite size and lack of arms, it was used in boudoirs as a perch on which a lady would sit and put on her slippers. Through the centuries, the slipper chair morphed and modernized into what is typically seen today: a boxy, armless upholstered chair that has both a low back and short legs.

It is designer Billy Baldwin who has been most associated with the slipper chair, having frequently used it in many clients' homes. A far cry from the feminine, curvy slipper chairs of yesteryear, Baldwin's masculine version was all straight lines and firmness with a squared-off low back, snug-fitting cushion, and a tailored skirt that hung to the ground, hiding the chair's legs. Still today, Baldwin's slipper chair seems to be the one most preferred by designers. But not all designers took such a rigorous approach to this chair. The early Hollywood film star turned decorator William Haines was known for his hostess chair. A riff on the

Although its origin as a delicate lady's chair dates back to eighteenth-century Europe, the slipper chair is today most associated with Billy Baldwin, whose signature version was similar to the one seen here.

IT IS DESIGNER BILLY BALDWIN WHO HAS
BEEN MOST ASSOCIATED WITH THE SLIPPER
CHAIR, HAVING FREQUENTLY USED IT IN MANY
CLIENTS' HOMES.

slipper chair, the hostess chair had a padded curved back, low seat, and in typical Hollywood fashion, showy legs that lacked a skirt.

Despite its origins in the boudoir, the slipper chair seems made for entertaining, its lack of arms and short back allowing one to converse from all sides. Baldwin and Haines must have thought so, too, since both designers used slipper chairs in their clients' party-ready living and drawing rooms. Its small profile is also an asset when it comes to furniture placement, allowing the slipper chair to be situated in spots where larger chairs just won't fit. Try placing a pair of small slipper chairs on either side of a cocktail table or together, facing the sofa, for a compact seating arrangement.

Remember the old-fashioned advice that petite people shouldn't wear too much pattern as it might overwhelm them? Well, the same holds true for the slipper chair. A solid-colored fabric looks best, although a subtle pattern could be used. And whether you choose to expose your chair's legs or not is up to you, but a skirt or bullion fringe will provide a suitable cover-up in rooms where there are already too many legs showing.

SEE ALSO
Passementerie.

STENCILS

"RUSTIC" AND "HOMESPUN" ARE TWO WORDS THAT SOMETIMES come to mind when people's thoughts turn to stencils. Indeed, early Americans and later the Pennsylvania Dutch stenciled their homes' walls and furniture with motifs of flowers, hearts, and pineapples in an effort to cheer up their typically austere interiors. But just as interior design has come a long way since America's early days, so too have stencils, with practically every style and pattern now appearing on these decorative templates.

Because of their stylistic range, stencils provide practical antidotes to any number of design problems. Let's say you have a room whose walls lack crown molding. You could hire a carpenter to install wood trim, but that could be a costly endeavor. Instead, consider using a stencil perforated with a fretwork or Greek key pattern, for example, to create a painted border at the tops of your walls. Pale blue walls crowned with a Chinese-red fretwork border look chic, as do gray walls topped with navy-blue Greek key trim. In fact, there are all kinds of architectural stencils, from those that imitate columns to some that mimic paneling, that can be used to embellish walls whose architecture is lacking.

Have you ever wished that you could match your dining room walls to your dinner china? Well, you can if your china is the classic Blue

SEE ALSO
Paneled Walls.

Willow pattern. The Stencil Library, a British-based website that carries scores of beautiful stencils (including the previously mentioned architectural versions), has just the pattern for you: Willow Pattern. Don't fret if your china is embellished with hyacinths, phlox, pheasants, ducks, shells, or acanthus leaves, because the Stencil Library has stencils that will coordinate with those patterns too.

Furniture can also benefit from the aid of stencils. Back in the 1930s and 1940s, it was not uncommon to see a lady's bedroom decorated in the French style, with a single fabric, often a floral print, used throughout the room for curtains, upholstery, bed canopies, bed coverlets and skirts, and even the walls. Sometimes this same print would be painted onto bureaus and dressing tables using custom-cut stencils. The effect was utterly charming and feminine, and it is one that you should consider for your own bedroom, especially if you have found a printed fabric with which you're particularly smitten.

Stencils, especially those bearing single motifs like stars, arrows, swags, and urns, can help to enrich all kinds of surfaces, like doors, cabinetry, floors, and even textiles. In one of her show house rooms, designer Bunny Williams placed a sisal rug that had been hand-painted with a geometric border and a sprinkling of stars, an idea that you could duplicate with a star-patterned stencil and the appropriate paint.

Through the addition of both stenciled and freehand-painted embellishments, a wheel-back chair radiates liveliness and charm, especially when partnered with a solid fabric seat.

*Bold red and white stripes present a snappy backdrop
for an ornate mirror and curvy table—a dazzling vignette
that would have made Dorothy Draper swoon.*

STRIPED WALLS

CLEAN, CRISP STRIPES CAN BE SO VISUALLY SATISFYING, ESPECIALLY to those of us who prefer order and structure in our lives and our homes. Think of all the marvelous things that are made even more special thanks to stripes: from the iconic brown-and-white Henri Bendel shopping bag to the ubiquitous striped canvas awnings that pepper the Côte d'Azur.

Of course, the same goes for walls, where stripes not only add flair but have the power to transform as well, making rooms with low ceilings appear taller than they really are. Narrow rooms can also benefit from stripes, especially if the stripes run horizontally across a room's walls so as to add some visual girth to the space. (This same optical illusion is the reason why most of us avoid wearing horizontal lines, lest we end up looking broader than we really are.)

Many of the great designers saw the virtues of striped walls, and none more so than Dorothy Draper. Draper preferred her stripes in shades of pink, green, or black against white backgrounds, but the common denominator was that her stripes were always at least five inches wide, never less. Keep the five-inch rule in mind if you plan to paint or paper your walls in gutsy colored stripes. Otherwise you might end up feeling like a caged animal in your striped room.

SEE ALSO
*Floral and
Foliage Prints;
Toiles.*

One of the chicest kitchens that I've ever seen was in a 1940s-era photograph of designer Frances Elkins's San Francisco home. Both the walls *and* ceiling were papered in hefty gold-and-white stripes, something that imparted some glamour to the room's rather ho-hum-looking kitchen appliances. So as to not interrupt the walls' patterned effect, Elkins even chose a striped window shade as well. And all of this in a room that supposedly was rarely used!

Stripes can be subtle, too, yet have just as much personality as their more exuberant cousins. Walls covered in whisper-thin stripes in muted, neutral tones impart a French Empire feel to a room, especially if a matching fabric is used for curtains and upholstery. There are also some striking-looking, solid-colored papers whose striped effect is achieved through alternating bands of matte and glossy finishes. Subtle, yet sophisticated.

And don't forget that stripes can be quite versatile, partnering well with floral prints, toiles, and other loosely rendered prints that help to counteract the stripes' severity. Then there's the all-American combination of stars and stripes, a pairing that will look patriotically chic forever.

THE DOROTHY DRAPER LOOK

Striped walls were to Dorothy Draper (1889–1969) what spaghetti is to meatballs—you just can't imagine one without the other. But bold beefy stripes alone did not define Draper's interiors. Other hallmarks of the Draper look include:

- Black-and-white patterned floors
- Plaster ornamentation
- Baroque flourishes
- Graphic color combinations
- Large glossy lampshades
- Oversize doors
- Cabbage-rose chintz

SUNBURST MOTIFS

THE MOST REGAL OF ALL DECORATIVE FLOURISHES HAS TO BE THE sunburst motif. It's the Sun King himself, Louis XIV of France, whom we have to thank for this heliocentric motif, one that traditionally depicted rays of the sun emanating from the face of Apollo. Intended as a symbol of the Sun King's supremacy, the sunburst motif adorned furnishings and architecture from this era, thereby assuming a stately position in the history of design.

Just as interior decoration loosened up throughout the twentieth century, so, too, did the sunburst motif. For the most part, gone was the face of Apollo. The sunburst became a more graphic, geometric version of its former self, one that now resem-bled its closely related cousin, the starburst motif (which, as the name implies, looks like an exuberantly twinkling star). No longer relegated to a world of gilded grandeur, the sunburst emblem adorned Art

A favorite embellishment of Art Deco designers, the sunburst motif is often seen fashioned into clocks and mirrors, both of which lend regal bearing to the rooms over which they preside.

WHETHER THE MOTIF IS FOUND ON FABRIC
OR WALLPAPER, THE SUNBURST ADDS A NOTE
OF ENERGY AND VITALITY TO AN INTERIOR.

Deco furniture and 1930s-era floors, though in a stylized way. Affordable versions of sunburst-style mirrors and clocks, sometimes made of gold-painted plastic, became popular decorative accessories and remain so today.

What makes the sunburst motif so appealing is that it is dynamic thanks to those radiating bursts of sun rays. Whether the motif is found on fabric or wallpaper (like Cole & Son's Il Sole, part of the Fornasetti collection), the sunburst adds a note of energy and vitality to an interior, and it also helps to draw attention to whatever it embellishes. It's also worth noting that the sunburst is a motif that never goes out of style and that almost always looks tasteful, meaning that you can hang that sunburst mirror on your wall without fear of it looking gauche.

The most fervent twentieth-century interpreter of the sunburst motif, though, had to be the aforementioned Piero Fornasetti, the late Italian designer who made the motif a hallmark of his work. Applied to tables, ashtrays, dinner plates, and screens, Fornasetti's suns were notable for their human-like faces and geometric rays. At times, the designer even partnered his suns with their old counterpart, the moon. Considering that much of Fornasetti's work dates back to a half century ago, it's impressive how fresh it still looks today.

TABLESCAPES

CONTRARY TO CURRENT POPULAR BELIEF, THE WORD *TABLESCAPE* was not coined by television food personality Sandra Lee, but rather by David Hicks, the esteemed British decorator. Hicks's skill at crafting tabletop assemblages or, to use another Hicks phrase, table landscapes, was so exceptional that designers still look to his work for inspiration some forty years later.

What made Hicks's tablescapes so memorable? First, they looked balanced, with a visually appealing blend of height and scale. Under Hicks's watchful eye, tall or hefty pieces such as lamps or tabletop statues provided counterpoints to small objects like decorative boxes, which prevented the grouping from appearing too bulky or, alternatively, too puny. Also, contrasting and, at times, wildly disparate objects looked harmonious when Hicks grouped them together, because of clever juxtaposition. It's a little like the theory that opposites attract, but in Hicks's case, it was the interplay of the highbrow grouped with the mundane, texture placed next to polish, and something rustic partnered with something sleek that transformed each piece into the extraordinary.

These tricks might sound a little esoteric and even complicated, but arranging a successful tablescape doesn't have to be difficult. Start off with simple arrangements and, in time, you'll be an old pro like

Hicks. If you recall, a collection should be grouped en masse. Take a small collection of objects that you have, like sterling silver powder compacts, and place them on a table. Because compacts lie practically flat against the table's surface, you will need to create some depth to your tablescape by introducing a lamp, an obelisk or two, or a porcelain *tulipière*, all of which are good choices for adding height and dimension to this arrangement. Think about the finish of your compacts. Their polished shine needs to be balanced by something textural, which could be a coarse linen tablecloth or a piece of rough-cut marble. Because sterling silver can look a little fancy, place something in the mix that has an unassuming charm, like a small vase of wildflowers or perhaps a chipped piece of antique Delftware. And there you have it. A tablescape in which the table's whole is truly greater than the sum of its parts.

Keep in mind that table landscapes don't have to be symmetrical like garnitures. In fact, tablescapes that lack symmetry are more appealing than those that appear forced and fussy. While sofa side tables, cocktail tables, and console tables can each benefit from tablescapes, it's best not to crowd every table in a room with such assemblages. Give your eye a place to rest by leaving some surfaces minimally decorated. Otherwise there will simply be too many objects to take in. And don't forget that tablescapes can and should be changed at whim. After all, accessorizing your tabletops is a far easier way to transform the look of your room than painting the walls or hanging curtains.

SEE ALSO
*Collections;
Garnitures;
Skirted Tables.*

In this carefully arranged tablescape, a tall lamp is grounded by stacks of books, while the dog sculpture's fluid lines harmonize with the surrounding straight angles. A mixture of materials was used, including wood, metal, and ceramics.

215

TENTED ROOMS

TENTED ROOMS, THOSE ILLUSIONARY SPACES DESIGNED TO EMULATE the inside of a tent, can trace their popularity back to Napoléon's reign, an era that, thanks to frequent military campaigns, saw the French leader and his officers lending French savoir faire to the battlefield through dashing tents and modish campaign furniture. Macho must never have looked so chic, because French designers of the 1950s and 1960s, especially Madeleine Castaing, followed suit, stylishly tenting their clients' rooms with typical French aplomb.

Creating a tented room of one's own requires military precision, but because the result is so luxurious and cosseting, a feather in your home's cap, any exertion of effort is worthwhile. Just like a real tent, both the walls and ceiling of your tented space must be covered in the same fabric or wallpaper to get the full effect. Although stripes are a classic choice for tented rooms (in homage to those striped ticking tents used by Napoléon), any print or solid can be used. If you choose fabric, either upholster the room's walls in the material or simply hang the fabric from the walls' tops, allowing it to hang in loose folds or bunching it tightly in shirred-type fashion.

The ceiling, however, is the tricky part, as it must give the illusion of the top of a pitched tent. Billowy fabric draped from the ceiling's

This striped tented room harks back to Napoléon's military tents, while its scalloped cornice softens the stripes' severity. Yellow and black was a color combination frequently seen in tented rooms of the 1960s and '70s.

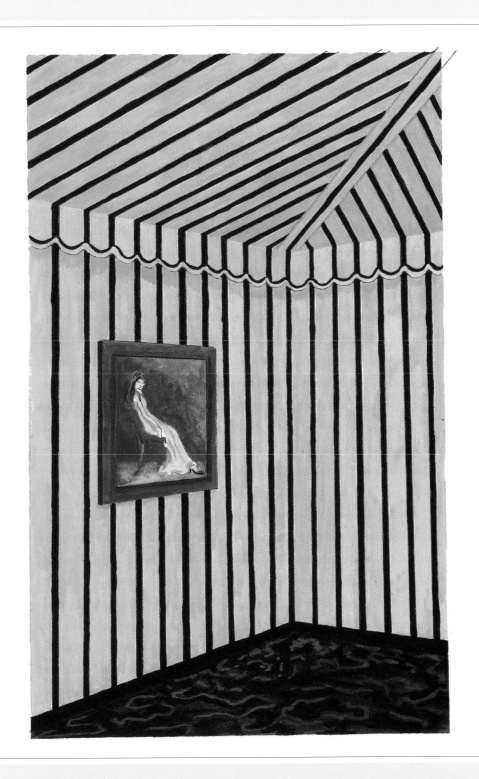

SEE ALSO
Canopied Beds;
Passementerie;
Tented Rooms.

nature keeps grandiosity at bay, creating a warm and welcoming home. And when acting as a backdrop for steely, contemporary accents, this fabric strikes a comforting note, warming up modernism's sometimes cold exterior.

This bedroom is lavished in ticking, including its headboard, bed curtain, table skirt, and even the curtain holdbacks. Because the stripe is so subtle, the bedroom remains a soothing space.

To witness ticking's versatility in action, we need look no further than the homes of Carolina Herrera Jr., daughter of fashion designer Carolina Herrera. A devotee, like her mother, of ticking by British fabric house Ian Mankin, Herrera chose the fabric for her dreamy Spanish estancia, where it was used for comfortable upholstery on a Spanish Empire daybed as well as for carefree-looking curtains. And in Herrera's snappy Madrid apartment, ticking was draped over her bed as a jaunty bed canopy. Few fabrics are as effective or as appropriate in both town and country.

Ticking, however, has not forgotten its modest background. Because it remains affordable compared with other fabrics, it's the thrifty choice for projects like tented rooms or upholstered walls that require a lavish amount of fabric.

 SUMMERTIME, AND THE LIVIN' IS EASY

Mark Hampton was a firm believer that come warm weather, homeowners should decorate their abodes in "summer garb" that includes ticking slipcovers, bare floors, and cheery plants and flowers. Indeed, lightweight fabrics go a long way to creating a retreat from the heat, but there are many other domestic details that embody those laid-back, carefree days of summer:

- Brightly colored cotton table mats and napkins that don't require ironing
- Cotton voile bed sheets, like those from D. Porthault
- Terra-cotta pots of scarlet, fuchsia, and pale-pink Geraniums

- Cotton throw rugs scattered throughout the house
- Batik print fabrics
- Ceiling fans whirring on porches and in sunrooms
- Fill-in invitations embossed with crabs, shells, or sailboats

TOBACCIANA

FOR MUCH OF THE TWENTIETH CENTURY, SMOKING WAS DEPICTED in a glamorous light, especially in the movies. Think of Audrey Hepburn's Holly Golightly and her extraordinarily long cigarette holder in *Breakfast at Tiffany's*. Or how about that romantically charged scene in the 1942 film classic *Now, Voyager*, in which actor Paul Heinreid's character simultaneously lights two cigarettes in his mouth and then offers one to his love interest, played by Bette Davis. Davis's character is so overwrought with emotion, perhaps due to her paramour's seductive way with a cigarette, that she goes on to utter the film's most famous line, "Don't let's ask for the moon. We have the stars."

Once symbols of elegant entertaining in the mid-twentieth century, a vintage bone-china cigarette urn has been pressed into service as a small vase to hold flowers, while a matching ashtray holds dragées and other candies.

While the number of smokers might be dwindling, the area of collecting known as *tobacciana* is as popular as ever. Antique and vintage cigarette cases, lighters, ashtrays, and the like—all hallmarks of tobacciana—are coveted more for their looks than for their intended purposes. And high-style looks are what many of these old smoking accessories have. Cole Porter's wife, Linda, often celebrated the openings of her husband's Broadway shows by giving him custom cigarette cases made by famed jeweler Fulco di Verdura. Lighters could also be items of beauty, and none more so than those made by another celebrated jeweler, Jean Schlumberger, whose designs included an

SEE ALSO
*Collections;
Scented
Candles.*

eighteen-carat gold lighter crafted to look like a fish. Is it any wonder that collectors crave such trifles?

Illustrious provenances aside, vintage cigarette cases and boxes, especially those made of metals or gemstones, add flair to any table surface, where their presence serves to spark interest. If you have an assemblage of smoking accessories, polish them up and display them together on a living room side table or a bedroom dresser.

Tobacciana can be quite useful too. Take, for example, ashtrays, which are great for holding things. The larger trays can be used in one's bedroom or dressing room as *vide-poches* for jewelry, watches, and even eyeglasses. I'm partial to small ashtrays, particularly those made by Hermès, which I often use to hold a single matchbook. I then place it next to one of my scented candles so that I don't have to hunt for matches every time I want to light it.

Cigarette urns, typically made of sterling silver or bone china, were once fixtures on cocktail and dining tables. Although they were made to hold cigarettes, consider using them as small flower vases that can be scattered around a dining table or as sleek little receptacles for hors d'oeuvres picks. (You'll find a vast number of these urns for sale on both eBay and the Replacements websites.) Have you ever seen old photos of fancy dinner parties where small sterling ashtrays were placed at every table setting? If you ever come across a set of these ashtrays at an antiques store or tag sale, snap them up. They can still be used on the dinner table, this time around serving as small nut or candy dishes.

 TOILES

TOILE, THAT PRINTED COTTON FABRIC DEVELOPED IN EIGHTEENTH-century France, is a storied fabric, especially considering that its most notable feature was that there was always a charming allegorical scene repeated across it. Traditionally rendered in monochromatic colors such as blue, black, red, or green against a white background, toile's prints were quite detailed thanks to that century's advances in copperplate engraving, allowing these miniature allegories to be richly illustrative.

Formally known as *toile de Jouy* because of its origins in Jouy-en-Josas, France, toile's themes were often pastoral, celebrating the simple pleasures of the country life, although some marked historical events or prominent monuments. One of the most charming toiles to have been designed during this fabric's early days was that which commemorated the Montgolfier brothers' invention and subsequent flight of a hot-air balloon in 1783. With illustrations of these early balloons splashed across the fabric, this thematic toile is still available today through textile firms like Quadrille and its Ballon de Gonesse toile. A similar scene played out in 1927 when aviator Charles Lindbergh flew across the Atlantic Ocean in his airplane, an event that fascinated the world and, like the hot-air balloon flight centuries before, inspired a commemorative toile designed by Passaic Print Works.

SEE ALSO
Acrylic;
Parsons Tables.

Unlike many decorative flourishes, toile looks best in a gracious plenty. If you choose a toile for a room's curtains, don't stop there. Repeat the same toile for walls (look for wallpapers that feature toile prints), upholstered furniture, even lampshades. An exuberant bestowment of toile in a single room gives this delightful print a sense of robustness that sometimes is lacking in a solo application. British designer Christopher Leach recently took this soup-to-nuts approach in his bijou London flat, where his bedroom walls, ceiling, bed linens, and built-in cabinetry were all covered in a brown-and-white toile. Rather than seeming smothering, the generous use of toile created a most luxurious, cocoon-like effect.

Although toile is by nature a traditional print, it is also a chameleon, changing its personality depending on the context. An old-fashioned black-and-white toile suddenly becomes modern looking when paired with black painted walls. Without a doubt, that classic red-and-white pastoral toile is a well-suited partner for rustic antiques, but mix it with contemporary classics like an acrylic table or a black lacquered Parsons table and that toile appears invigorated, as if fresh new life has been breathed into it. And when interpreted in bright, acid colors or rendered tonally, such as boysenberry scenes against a pale-purple background, toiles appear very much in keeping with today's popularity of saturated color.

While many currently produced toiles show little deviation from their eighteenth-century ancestors, there are updated scenes available that tell far different stories. Glasgow, Scotland–based Timorous Beasties has designed a few cheeky toiles, including one that depicts some saucy goings-on in New York City. And if you care to show your civic pride, there is Town Toiles, known for its prints depicting the landmarks of towns such as Charleston, South Carolina, and Tampa, Florida.

Scalamandré's classic Asian-themed toile, "Pillement Toile," appears on this table's cloth as well as its dinner china, both of which are unexpected places to see this traditional print, which usually graces curtains and wallpapers.

T | TÔLE

TÔLE, A TRADITIONAL CRAFT IN WHICH TIN OBJECTS ARE DECORA-
tively painted, could be described as a precursor to today's vogue for
repurposing and recycling, that is, if you believe one historical tale. In
late eighteenth-century Europe, tea was often sold in sizable tin canisters that, rather than being discarded once empty, were given new
decorative life thanks to painted veneers and embellishments. Usually painted by the lady of the house, these tea canisters could then be
used throughout the house, later being joined by other tin accessories
to form a new handicraft, tôle, which became popular among gentle-
women of that era.

Most antique tôle typically bears a black painted background,
although red, green, and yellow were also deemed acceptable colors,
while decoration often included Asian, Empire, or neoclassical motifs
mostly rendered in gold paint. In addition to tea canisters, metal candle shades (like those designed for bouillotte lamps), planters, desk
accessories, and even dustpans were all decoratively painted in the tôle
style, befitting for a craft that was informal in manner. In fact, much
new tôle bears a striking resemblance to its antique predecessors, with
similar forms being painted in much the same manner as they were
centuries ago.

*A tôle tray,
which is richly
painted with
Chinese figures
against a black
background,
is so highly
decorative
that little else
is needed to
accessorize this
table's top.
Tôle trays are
also typically
hung on walls
as decoration.*

Although many decorative antiques can be used today in both traditional and contemporary settings, tôle remains an unapologetic holdout, one that seems more comfortable among conventional furniture pieces and down-to-earth fabrics than among sleek and sexy furnishings. In a room decorated with ticking or chintz and simple antique furniture, a tôle lamp or cachepot, for example, can be a homey touch, one that imbues a space with the charm of yesteryear. And don't forget

SEE ALSO
Bouillotte Lamps; Chintz; Sconces; Ticking.

about the tôle tray that, despite its frequent appearance as a wall hanging, is useful as the top of an ottoman coffee table or, when given a stand upon which to perch, as a tray table.

Bear in mind that while most tôle harkens back to the style of those archetypal tea canisters, there are some examples that break the mold. Midcentury Italian-made chandeliers and sconces festooned with metal leaves, flowers, or fruit are considered to be tôle because of their painted surfaces, as are those 1960s-era painted metal umbrella stands and trays designed by artist Piero Fornasetti. And remember the recent popularity of those painted metal trays that bear the legendary orange-and-brown logo of the famous French leather and fashion house? Those are tôle, too, although you might not have realized it at first glance.

T | TROMPE L'OEIL

TROMPE L'OEIL, THE FRENCH TERM FOR THE ARTISTIC CAPRICE whose sole purpose is to "deceive the eye," has both delighted and fooled people for centuries. Sometimes taking shape in porcelain (such as a tureen that appears as though a real head of lettuce) and at other times pictures (like those seventeenth-century Dutch oil paintings in which the subject's hands look as though they're reaching out, beyond the canvas's confines, toward the viewer), trompe l'oeil is at its most mischievous when appearing on a wall, an expansive canvas befitting such decorative tomfoolery.

Wallpaper designed in the trompe l'oeil style is, of course, the most uncomplicated manner in which to create an illusionary effect, requiring no artist other than a paper hanger. There are wallpapers that mimic button tufting, giving walls the impression that they're upholstered (Cheryl by Rose Cumming by Dessin Fournir), as well as draped fabric hanging on a wall (Thibaut's Drapery wallpaper). Architecture, too, can be conjured up using trompe l'oeil wallpaper, including balustrade wainscoting, a colonnade of columns, or even a wall façade of bricks.

Books, or more specifically, their spines, have long been a popular ruse in trompe l'oeil's bag of tricks. In the library at Chatsworth, the English manse of the Duke and Duchess of Devonshire, there is a jib

This bedroom's walls might appear to be upholstered and tufted in pink fabric, but, in truth, they are papered in trompe l'oeil wallpaper by Rose Cumming by Dessin Fournir. Similar wallpaper was seen frequently in French interiors during the 1950s and '60s.

The late Nan Kempner raised the style quotient of the tray dinner immensely when she incorporated a Lucite TV tray, one that lacked a foldable base, into a fantasy table setting created for Tiffany & Co. Of course, the fact that Kempner's tray was set with Flora Danica, the most coveted and expensive of all china patterns, didn't hurt. TV trays even got the presidential seal of approval when Ronald and Nancy Reagan were once photographed supping from a pair of trays in the White House!

The answer to taking your dinner on a TV tray is to create as attractive a table setting as possible. After all, eating one's Caesar salad or moo shu pork from a takeout container can make for a lackluster dining experience. Lay down a linen or cotton place mat with matching napkin and use your nice stainless or sterling flatware. Drink your water or iced tea from a goblet, or if you prefer wine, bring a small carafe of it to your tray so that you don't have to get up for refills. The point is to spoil yourself, so treat your tray meal as a dinner party for one.

And as much as we might associate these tray tables with dining in front of the telly, we mustn't discount their other uses. A TV tray works well as an impromptu serving table for hors d'oeuvres or glasses of wine. Or why not employ one as an effortless yet chic occasional table? They don't take up much room and can be placed anywhere. Even in Diana Vreeland's famous "Garden in Hell" living room, there was a small folding table that held an ashtray and matches, but unless you're a smoker, you could use your tray to hold books, a collection of porcelain, or even a potted plant. Much like the number of cable channels, the options are plentiful for your TV tray.

SEE ALSO
Acrylic; Faux Finishes; Malachite; Occasional Tables.

Dining from a TV tray doesn't mean you have to skimp on your table setting. A linen mat and napkin, an individual tureen shaped as a tiny pink cabbage, and a small wine carafe make a weeknight meal seem like a Saturday night dinner party.

U | UPHOLSTERED DOORS

"DOORS ARE USUALLY ORPHANS—NOBODY PAYS ATTENTION TO them," wrote Dorothy Draper, a designer who rarely missed an architectural moment upon which to make a splashy statement. Draper's declaration rings true, as a room's walls, windows, and floors tend to receive the lion's share of the decoration with the overlooked door playing second fiddle. It's time to right this wrong by lavishing the door with attention, and few decorative gestures are as chic as the upholstered door.

Upholstered blue leather dresses up what would otherwise be a banal swinging door. Paneling, which was loosely based on a Dorothy Draper— designed door, is implied through nickel nailhead trim.

If you're a fan of British literature or *Masterpiece Theatre*, you're probably familiar with the infamous "green baize door." A once-standard feature in English upper-class houses, the baize door was a swinging door, typically positioned between the house's pantry and dining room. The door was covered in a woolen fabric known as *baize,* for which the traditional color choice was green. Baize-upholstered doors muffled sounds of footmen coming and going during meal service and prevented cooking odors from entering the dining room, thus ensuring a genteel experience for the family of the house. But the green baize door also became a very real symbol of the social delineation between those who worked "below stairs" (the staff, including the housekeeper, butler, and lady's maid) and the wealthy family who lived "above stairs."

Although the days of *Upstairs, Downstairs* are over, the baize door lives on in a more democratic fashion. Upholstered doors are no longer limited to service quarters like kitchens and butler's pantries, although these rooms still see their fair share of such doors. Today, in addition, the doors leading to powder rooms, hall closets, libraries, dressing rooms, and even bedrooms can benefit from such embellishment, their fabric-covered surfaces serving as luxurious buffers between rooms. And while the pivoting, or swinging, door is the most classic example of all upholstered doors, really, most doors can be swathed in fabric.

Speaking of fabric, leather has become a favorite covering for doors thanks to its supple good looks and durability. With such colorful animal hides now available from companies like Moore & Giles and Edelman Leather, you can indulge your door in shades like teal, cerise, or chartreuse, if you wish. Traditional baize, felt, and wool fabrics, especially in red or green, continue to be applied to many doors, especially in rooms where they should be subtle, not showy. You can even wrap your door in silk, but this fabric is best left to minimally handled doors. Don't forget that if your upholstered door is one that swings, you'll need to buy a glass push plate, available at hardware stores and websites, that can be attached to the door over its fabric or leather layer. That way, hands have a protective surface upon which to open the door, keeping its fabric front from appearing manhandled.

And few upholstered doors really look complete without the use of nailhead trim, which goes a long way to giving the door a finished appearance. Nailheads can outline door fronts, imply architectural paneling, or even mimic an intricate pattern. With such a surfeit of attention, your home's doors will no longer look, or feel, abandoned.

V VALANCES

WITH SO MANY PEOPLE NOW FORGOING PROPER WINDOW VALANCES, it could be said, to borrow designer Michael Greer's quip, that "everybody seems to have lost his sense of valance." What a shame, considering that valances, those fabric treatments made to crown the tops of windows, not only dress up windows but serve a practical purpose too.

As visual sleights-of-hand, valances can disguise architectural problems. Say your room has short windows that leave wide gaps of wall space

above them. To "raise" the windows and make them appear taller than they are, add valances that just barely hide the tops of your windows but that reach up to the ceiling. People will simply assume that your "statuesque" windows extend up behind those valances. What about walls that are plagued with windows of varying height? Have valances made of the same height, ones that will barely lap at the tops of the short windows but that will inevitably cover up the head and shoulders of the tall windows. The visual effect will be one of harmony, as if all of the room's windows are identical.

Behaving much like a hat or, at times, an elaborate coiffure, a valance crowns the window and curtains beneath it, bestowing finish, flair, and prominence to the entire window ensemble.

SEE ALSO
Passementerie.

These window toppers, which by the way, are usually used in conjunction with curtains or shades, also mask window hardware like curtain rods or blind brackets that shouldn't be seen. Such practicality notwithstanding, it's a valance's looks that really make this window treatment the charmer it is. Because valances are loosely constructed, they can be plied into soft folds or swags, pleats, or even pennants that, as the name suggests, look like little pointy flags. Valances can also be flourished with fringe, ribbon tape, or other types of passementerie. And while valances can, of course, be made of the same fabric as that of their underlying curtains or shades, they don't have to. In my childhood dining room, the windows had blue silk valances and Chinese red Venetian blinds, a contrasting window scheme that was quite pretty.

If you prefer a valance that has more structure to it, consider the *pelmet*, which is basically a valance that, because it is stiffened, is shapely. Pelmets can be made to resemble the tops of pagodas, arches, or even, with big rounded corners, Princess Leia's side buns. The shape of a pelmet can be accentuated with trim applied along the pelmet's perimeter. But bear in mind that because pelmets have more architectural heft than soft valances, they should be in keeping with a home's interior architecture. In the designer John Fowler's country house, the Hunting Lodge, the structure's Gothick details (an eighteenth-century adaption of traditional Gothic architecture) were mimicked in a set of window pelmets shaped in pointy Gothic arches. Wouldn't they have looked silly had they been, say, Moorish arches?

Of course, some people have gone past the point of no return, likening the valance to their also-on-the-wane clothing counterpart, the hat. But just like the hat, a valance adds finish to a window's outfit; it is the crowning touch that transforms your windows from ho-hum to gorgeous.

VEGETABLE AND FRUIT CERAMICWARE

WHAT DID BROOKE ASTOR, THE DUCHESS OF WINDSOR, JACQUELINE Kennedy, C.Z. Guest, and many other prominent ladies have in common? Well, among other things, a taste for vegetables and fruits, specifically those of the ceramic kind.

Ceramicware modeled after vegetables and fruit has a long tradition in the decorative arts, with some of the more sought after examples being eighteenth- and nineteenth-century French faience as well as English or Italian majolica. The Musée des Arts Décoratifs in Paris has an enviable collection of these ceramics, including an eggplant that looks so real, you want to take a bite out of it! Many types of fruits and vegetables have been rendered in clay, including bundles of asparagus tied up in ribbons, heads of cabbage and cauliflower, artichokes, and melons, to name just a few. While some of this ceramicware was created solely for decorative purposes, much was crafted into tureens, bowls, boxes, and platters for use on the table.

One of the more popular and collectible types of ceramics is cabbage ware, formed to resemble its vegetal namesake. Usually painted in to-be-expected green, cabbage ware includes plates composed of single cabbage leaves, bowls that resemble small cupped leaves, and tureens that can look like the spitting images of real heads of cabbage. The most

SEE ALSO
Trompe L'oeil.

coveted, not to mention expensive, of all cabbage ware was that made by Florida potter Dodie Thayer, although her pieces were modeled after lettuce rather than cabbage. Thayer's lettuce ware pieces included tureens (which go for thousands of dollars today at auction), sugar bowls and creamers, platters, vases, teapots, butter pats, and, well, I really could go on and on. Suffice it to say, Thayer produced a bumper crop of lettuce-like ceramics.

Another favorite form is trompe l'oeil plates that look as though real fruits or vegetables have been placed on them. Most porcelain fruits and vegetables look awfully close to the real thing, but what these trompe l'oeil plates have going for them is a heightened realism, as if someone had placed an orange or pear, for example, on a plate in anticipation of eating it. The other purpose behind such plates is that they can be placed upon a stack of dinner plates, say, on a buffet table, where their presence adds a witty and finishing touch. And speaking of humor, try placing a small plate of trompe l'oeil black olives or walnuts on a living room side table and watch as your guests attempt to eat one.

These white plates have ceramic walnuts and hazelnuts attached to them in the trompe l'oeil style. Made by the Italian factory, Este, they are highly sought after by collectors who prefer their modern looks to traditionally rendered fruits and vegetables.

Although a collection of porcelain fruits or vegetables can look traditional and ladylike (not bad adjectives in my book), they don't have to. Consider how Tiffany & Co.'s late design director Van Day Truex displayed his trompe l'oeil vegetable plates, which, by the way, became popular after Truex introduced them at Tiffany's in the 1960s. Placed against the plain, textured plaster walls in his elegantly minimal French country house, the plates lost any potential cuteness thanks to their sober backdrop. If you're predisposed to thinking that this type of porcelain is saccharine, an incongruous placement of your porcelain fruits and veggies will go a long way to toning down the sweetness and making them easier to swallow.

VERRE ÉGLOMISÉ

SEE ALSO
Sconces;
Screens.

GLASS OF FASHION, A PHRASE ONCE WRITTEN BY SHAKESPEARE, might well be used to describe *verre églomisé*, the exquisite art form in which the underside of glass is gilded in mostly silver or gold leaf. The French term for "gilded glass," *verre églomisé* has been documented as far back as the thirteenth century, when it was used on pulpits in Italian churches. This gilded glass still plays a supporting role in design, one that enhances the furniture upon which it is applied.

Traditionally, *verre églomisé* has been incorporated into tables and screens and used to accent wall mirrors and sconces. In the 1930s *verre églomisé* really hit its glamorous stride, chosen by French designers like Jules Leleu for swank interiors. On the 1930s-era S.S. *Normandie*, the most luxuriously appointed of all ocean liners, *verre églomisé* panels were selected to adorn the ship's grand lounge, a fitting counterpart to the Lalique glass light fixtures and Christofle silver hollowware that also graced the ship's interiors.

A band of white and gold verre églomisé, *which depicts leaves, flowers, and ribbon, adds decorative interest to the bottom of this antique English pier mirror. Rather than gilding the lily, so to speak,* verre églomisé *imparts gleaming elegance.*

Luxurious is an apt description of *verre églomisé* because newly created pieces are quite expensive, a result of the skill and labor that this art form requires. But when your budget does allow for a piece or two, whether old or new, you should certainly take the plunge and purchase them, as few other types of decoration have such dramatic flair.

W | WHIMSY

ALTHOUGH IT'S DEFINED AS CAPRICIOUS, WHIMSY HAS LONG played an earnest role in design as a fanciful decorative gesture that adds lighthearted style to one's home. Those confident in their taste tend to appreciate whimsy, which might explain why the current Dowager Duchess of Devonshire chose to hang a portrait of Elvis, her long-time crush, on the silver foil–papered walls of her powder room or why Cecil Beaton encouraged his guests to trace the outline of their hands onto his bathroom wall.

One way to introduce whimsy into a room is with wallpaper or fabric that is embellished with novelty prints, those hard-to-categorize prints that include humorous, clever, and at times, slightly bizarre designs. Such whimsical prints include asparagus stalks woven into plaid (Brunschwig & Fils' fittingly named Asparagus Plaid), dogs driving vintage cars (Tyler Hall's cruisin'), and Staffordshire ceramic spaniels (Francie and Grover by Carleton Varney By The Yard). Dog prints, by the way, are always appropriate displays of whimsy. For a devil-may-care style of decorating, there is also Devil Paper by Waterhouse Wallhangings, a wallpaper that shows silhouetted figures frolicking, dancing, and generally raising Cain while devils float among them. That this print dates back to the nineteenth century shows, I think, that even our more

The minute you walk into this stylish couple's entry hall, you know that it's the home of dog lovers. Osborne & Little's whimsical wallpaper, "Best in Show," looks sophisticated when mixed with antique furniture and vibrant blue foo dogs.

worldly, sophisticated, and wise, one who, through time, has acquired a polish that is, well, sometimes lacking in an upstart young man.

SEE ALSO
Acrylic.

Traditionally, furniture has been crafted in all kinds of wood, like mahogany, cherry, oak, poplar, and pine, meaning that there exists a brown wood that should appeal to you. For wood finishes with great flair, there is the highly regarded *marquetry*, a furniture craft in which different shades of wood veneer are applied to a surface in a decorative pattern, as well as *wood inlay*, in which areas of wood are removed from a surface and then inlaid with different colored wood. And then there is *cerused*, or limed, oak, in which a white wax is applied over the wood to whiten, and thus emphasize, the oak's naturally prominent graining. Limed oak was all the rage during the 1920s and 1930s, used to great effect by designers like Jean-Michel Frank, and it is once again becoming popular due to its modern-looking and not-quite-so-brown appearance.

For all of its virtues, wood furniture works best today in moderation and when combined with modern elements. A dark wood chest, for example, will look balanced and fresh when flanked by two contemporary-looking chairs made of acrylic or metal. And beware of wedding yourself to only one type of wood. Too much of one variety might make your house look more like a furniture showroom and less like a home.

Because of its simple design, a secretary's honey-toned wood finish becomes the focal point. Wood inlay, noticeable on both the door fronts and around the drawers' edges, provides subtle decoration to an otherwise sober piece.

W | WUNDERKAMMERS

ONE OF DESIGN HISTORY'S MORE CURIOUS RELICS HAS TO BE THAT of the seventeenth- and eighteenth-century *wunderkammers,* or "wonder rooms" in German. In fact, *curious* and *relic* are both apt words to describe these rooms considering that they often housed curated collections of curiosities, something that gave rise to the more commonly known term "cabinets of curiosities."

To most seventeenth-century Europeans, much of the world was a mystery. With knowledge rather limited, it's not surprising that many wealthy Europeans, usually those with an intellectual bent, sought to collect the tangible wonders of the world, objects that held fascination for all who viewed them. Nature's bounty like shells, rocks, and insect specimens could often be found in *wunderkammers,* as could fossils and taxidermy. Ancient relics and religious artifacts were present in many of these cabinets, as was the truly bizarre, such as preserved animal embryos.

Today, traditional *wunderkammers* don't seem quite as wondrous. That piece of coral so coveted by the eighteenth-century

An accessory that pays homage to Mother Nature, much like this illustrated bird's nest cradling alabaster eggs, evokes the spirit and curiosity of those legendary seventeenth- and eighteenth-century wunder-kammers.

collector has become more commonplace today, though no less beautiful, thanks to commercial travel and online shopping. And those morbid artifacts that were once nonpareil? They're best left in the seventeenth century. But it's the purpose of the *wunderkammer,* that which bestows pride of place upon objects of wonder, that still holds appeal. Although we may no longer have the space nor even the desire to devote a room or a cabinet to a collection of the unusual, a token of nature or a historical relic on display lends an element of rarity to our homes and indulges our desire to marvel.

Open your eyes to what nature offers up and you'll find myriad wonderments that will make darn good-looking decorative accessories too. Perhaps you have found an abandoned bird's nest in your yard. Why not place it on your entry hall console or living room side table and make it even more special by nestling alabaster eggs within it? That starfish that you found on the beach will find a fitting new home when placed on top of a stack of books. And what about a silver dish filled with acorns, one of the benefits of having an oak tree on your property?

Not all curiosities require you to be the cultivator, especially considering that there are a number of designers and shops that specialize solely in natural and embellished curios. Years ago, Arthur Court, the designer now better known for metal tableware, popularly took brightly colored minerals and geodes and mounted them on stylish little display stands. Today, it's Creel and Gow, one of New York's most fascinating shops, which prominently deals in the curious, including beautiful shells dipped in sterling silver, chunks of amber, and taxidermy. And then there's the venerable Deyrolle, the Paris-based holy grail of taxidermy that is on most designers' Paris to-do lists. Considering the continued popularity of taxidermy and other curiosities, it seems that the more things change, the more they actually stay the same.

Y | YARDAGE

EMBARK ON A FEW DECORATING PROJECTS IN YOUR HOME, AND inevitably you end up with leftover fabric yardage that is not quite enough to upholster, say, a sizable chair but is more than you can discard without feeling wasteful. To assuage those guilty feelings, there are all kinds of uses for this yardage that, thank heavens, don't require much expense or sewing expertise.

Many chairs, stools, and small benches have seats that can be easily lifted out of their frames for upholstering, and thus they make worthy recipients of your leftover fabric. With the aid of a staple gun, you can simply wrap the cushion in the fabric, staple it to the seat's underside, and pop it back into its frame. For an upholstery job that takes all of five minutes, your chairs and stools will be completely transformed. It's also an effective way to repeat the same fabric used elsewhere in a room, heightening the visual impact of, say, your patterned curtain fabric.

Gracious living calls for those discreet decorative touches that perhaps only you know are there but that add immensely to your day-to-day comfort. Perhaps you have enough fabric left over from your upholstered headboard project to line the drawers of your bureau. Cut squares of fabric to fit the dimensions of the drawers, and then adhere it to their bottoms using double-sided tape. The same idea can also be

Although my DIY skills are generally lacking, I am capable of making fragrance sachets out of leftover fabric yardage. Not only are these sachets very easy to sew together, but they are also a practical way to scent and beautify my closet.

Clark Gable, Gary Cooper, and Lana Turner, all of whom came to see and be seen . . . and perhaps swill champagne too. Lucky for those of us who were not El Morocco habitués, a comparable blue-and-white zebra print can still be had today: Zebrine by Rose Cumming by Dessin Fournir.

In fact, one of the assets of zebra prints is that they don't require a literal translation. Zebra stripes now come in a variety of perky shades, from Inca gold or shrimp (China Seas' Nairobi linen fabric) to violet or raspberry (both found in Duralee's fabric collection). And rather than being relegated to rough-and-tumble fabrics, zebra prints have been given refined terrains upon which to roam, from Jim Thompson's elegant silks to Brunschwig & Fils' classic silk velvets. Zebras certainly never looked so dapper.

The most famous of all zebra prints (and currently one of the most popular) has to be Scalamandré's Zebra wallpaper. Originally designed in the 1940s for use in the late, lamented Italian restaurant Gino in Manhattan, Scalamandré's wallpaper features zebras wearing their stripes, caught in midleap with arrows whizzing past them. Still sold today, the paper comes in a range of colored backgrounds, including black, gold, blue, and the original red, a shade that I assume helped to hide any spaghetti sauce splatters.

Jim Thompson's "Illusion," a yellow-and-silver-zebra-print silk ikat, provides this porter's chair with polished vigor while not interfering with the chair's prominent shape.

Linen

D. PORTHAULT
470 Park Avenue
New York, New York
212-688-1660
www.dporthault.com

**GRAMERCY FINE LINENS &
FURNISHINGS**
2351 A Peachtree Road
Atlanta, Georgia 30305
404-846-9244
www.shopgramercy.com

KASSATLY'S
250 Worth Avenue
Palm Beach, Florida 33480
800-655-9599
www.kassatlys.com

LEONTINE LINENS
800-876-4799
www.leontinelinens.com

LÉRON
979 Third Avenue, Suite 1521
New York, New York 10022
212-753-6700
www.leron.com

Passementerie and Ribbon

HOULÈS
www.houles.com

JANET YONATY INC.
www.janetyonaty.com

NICHOLAS KNIEL
www.nicholaskniel.com

THE RIBBONERIE
www.ribbonerie.com

SAMUEL & SONS
www.samuelandsons.com

Porcelain and Silver

BARDITH LTD.
901 Lexington Avenue
New York, New York 10021
212-737-3775
www.bardith.com

JAMES ROBINSON
480 Park Avenue
New York, New York 10022
752-6166
www.jrobinson.com

VIEUXTEMPS PORCELAIN
706-672-1144
www.vieuxtempsporcelain.net

Scenic and Historical Wallpaper

ADELPHI PAPER HANGINGS
www.adelphipaperhangings.com

DE GOURNAY
www.degournay.com

FROMENTAL
www.fromental.co.uk

GRACIE
www.graciestudio.com

ZUBER & CIE
www.zuber.fr

Stationery

DEMPSEY & CARROLL
www.dempseyandcarroll.com

PICKETT'S PRESS
www.pickettspress.com

THE PRINTERY
www.iprintery.com

ALEXA PULITZER
www.alexapulitzer.com

MRS. JOHN L. STRONG
www.mrsstrong.com

Tabletop and China

CHARLES WILLIS
465 East Paces Ferry Road
Atlanta, Georgia 30305
404-233-9487
800-883-4993
www.charleswillis.com

GUMP'S
135 Post Street
San Francisco, California 94108
415-982-1616
800-284-8677www.gumps.com

LETA AUSTIN FOSTER BOUTIQUE
64 Via Mizner
Palm Beach, Florida 33480
561-655-7367
www.letaaustinfosterboutique.com

MOTTAHEDEH
www.mottahedeh.com

REPLACEMENTS LTD.
www.replacements.com

SCULLY & SCULLY
504 Park Avenue
New York, New York 10022
212-755-2590
800-223-3717
www.scullyandscully.com

SUE FISHER KING
3067 Sacramento Street
San Francisco, California 94115
415-922-7276
www.suefisherking.com

TRAVADAVI
2300 Peachtree Road
Atlanta, Georgia 30309
404-844-0141
www.travadavi.com

ACKNOWLEDGMENTS

FIRST AND FOREMOST, I HAVE TO THANK MY PARENTS, JANICE AND Durelle Boles, for their support and encouragement, which has both sustained me through the years and propelled me down this winding road from design enthusiast to blogger to published author. From them, I learned that civility and a good education will carry one far in life.

I cannot think of anyone with whom I would rather collaborate than my sister, Laura Boles Faw, the best sister, friend, and illustrator one could ask for. Despite the fact that she's really a sculptor, she kindly allowed herself to be talked into illustrating a book for her big sister.

Thank goodness for my photographer, Erica George Dines, who brought not only her trained eye and loads of camera equipment to our photo shoots but also a sense of humor. Her talent and levity made shooting the photos for this book a pleasure.

This book might have always remained a dream were it not for my wonderful agent, William Clark, and my accomplished and enthusiastic editor at Clarkson Potter, Angelin Borsics. I couldn't have asked for two better champions. And a special thanks to the talented Clarkson Potter team of Rae Ann Spitzenberger, Jane Treuhaft, Terry Deal, Kim Tyner, Kim Small, and Carly Gorga, whose skill and hard work made my book something of which I am very proud.

It seems that anytime a career opportunity comes my way, Alexa Hampton somehow had a hand in it. I am fortunate to have Alexa as my fairy godmother, and I'm honored that she agreed to write the book's foreword.

I will be forever grateful to Stephen Drucker, Clinton Smith, and Newell Turner, all of whom believed in me from my earliest days of blogging. I have learned so much from each of these editors and can only hope that some of their talent rubs off on me.

I thank the following designers and homeowners, all of whom are dear friends, for allowing me to photograph their homes and projects for this book: Keith Arnold, Judy Bentley, Janice and Durelle Boles, Rory Carlton, David Coursey, Jean Davis, Heather Dewberry, Marc Ferguson, Scott Higley, Chad Holman, Will Huff, Barry Hutner, Jonathan Lacrosse, Barry Leach, Clinton Smith, and Keith Traxler.

I would also like to extend my thanks to the following friends and colleagues whose support and assistance were valuable in producing this book: Hal Ainsworth, Mario Buatta, Jean Caldwell, Louise Cronan, Sally Crouse, Alice Curtis, Michael Devine, Michael Dines, Matilda Dobbs, Emily Evans Eerdmans, Maureen Footer, Bebe Forehand, Chandler Grant, Duane Hampton, Harry Hinson, Florence Holmes, Jim Thompson fabrics, Janice Langrall, Adam Lewis, Victoria Manley, Ned Marshall, Will Merrill, Charlotte Moss, Lisa Newsom, Winton Noah, Parc Monceau Antiques, Angela Patrick, Kappy Powell, Danny Recoder, Miles Redd, Diane Dorrans Saeks, Holly Sawyer, Scalamandré fabrics and wallcoverings, Edward Schaefer, Lyn Schroeder, Kevin Sharkey, Michael Smith, Ruthie Sommers, Doretta Sperduto, Christopher Spitzmiller, Brian Spofford, Meredith Warnock, and Bunny Williams.

It seems appropriate to acknowledge my professors at my alma mater, the University of the South in Sewanee, Tennessee, particularly those in the history and English departments. Without their rigorous instruction, I wouldn't be the writer that I am today. Yea, Sewanee's Right!

And, finally, to all of you who read *The Peak of Chic,* I give you my heartfelt thanks. I have learned so much from you, and it is you who inspired me to write this book.